God is God. We are not. He ... face, this sounds depressing. ... is wonderfully freeing as it e ... everything to everyone, everyw...... I'm so glad Sean wrote this book!

JORDAN RAYNOR, national bestselling author of *Redeeming Your Time, Master of One,* and *Called to Create*

Sean McGever has been a lifelong bearer of good news. Here, he has done it again, this time proclaiming a refreshing declaration of freedom: "It's okay to be a human being!" Dietrich Bonhoeffer reminded us that we humans will always be limited in our understanding because we are creations. McGever has developed this idea and expanded it by encouraging us that part of being "beautifully and wonderfully made" (Ps. 139) by the Creator includes our limits. They are a part of the design, not a flaw. "It is for freedom that Christ has set us free" (Gal. 5:1).

SCOTT LISEA, campus pastor at Westmont College

McGever digs into the "hustle-pause spectrum" of our lives, emphasizing the reality of human limitation. According to McGever, our limitations do not pose a threat to kingdom work but are rather a reminder that God is King and we are his image bearers. I found much-needed purpose and relief in reading this book.

RACHEL JOY WELCHER, editor at *Fathom* magazine and author of *Talking Back to Purity Culture*

The Good News of Our Limits is a refreshing encouragement to embrace how God intentionally designed us as finite human beings. Through relatable stories and illustrations, McGever helps us all discover joy in our inadequacy.

DREW HILL, pastor and award-winning author of *Alongside: Loving Teenagers with the Gospel*

McGever leads us on a thought-provoking journey of self-discovery into the beautiful realizations of our God-given limitations. Along the path, he paints a relatable portrait filled with personal and familial anecdotes, helping readers find freedom through the knowledge of the limits of their humanity. This book makes a great gift for anyone needing to understand how they can flourish despite real inadequacies, through reliance in God and in community with fellow less-than-perfect believers.

SAMMY ALFARO, professor at College of
Theology, Grand Canyon University

In a culture that constantly tells us to do more, be more, work harder, and have success at all costs, this book provides a refreshing alternative way to live. We simply can't do it all. We need to learn how to listen to our lives, to recalibrate, and to make wise choices. Sean doesn't just write about this, he lives it. He is one of the most highly productive, effective leaders I know. Sean also lives out of a deep sense of his own unique gifting and a sense of clarity around the priorities of his life while acknowledging his own limits. This book is filled with practical stories and keen biblical insights that, if heeded, will be good and freeing news for all who read it.

PAM MOORE, senior director of learning
and leadership at Young Life

Rarely is a person as invested in the lives of adolescents and also committed to theological excellence as Sean. He is passionate about "being there" for a generation of kids who have struggled to find their way amid the pandemic. The mental health toll on teens and young adults has been devastating. The words in this book encourage people to receive the grace they need to be whole again and to be free from expectations of performance. Sean shows us that Scripture can free us, not get us caught up in the dos and don'ts of behavior that can be so discouraging. The freedom we have in Jesus rings loud and clear through Sean's words.

JAN HAMILTON, psychiatric nurse practitioner,
founder, and CEO of Doorways

No matter where you are in life, family, career, or your walk with Christ, the words scripted in *The Good News of Our Limits* will speak volumes to you. When the gospel says one person plants the seeds, another waters, and God creates the growth, I never really saw the perspective of this approach even though I had read this many times. *The Good News of Our Limits* provides a much-needed perspective of what God intends for us to do as opposed to us trying to be and do more than what is humanly possible.

WARREN PANICO, CEO of Sigma US

THE
GOOD NEWS
OF OUR
LIMITS

THE
GOOD NEWS
OF OUR
LIMITS

FIND GREATER PEACE, JOY,

AND EFFECTIVENESS THROUGH

GOD'S GIFT OF INADEQUACY

SEAN MCGEVER

**ZONDERVAN
REFLECTIVE**

CONTENTS

FOREWORD

E arly in my life, one of the biggest choices I had to make was picking my college major. Numerous topics interested me, and there were many things I wanted to do with my life, so narrowing it all down to only one choice was difficult. I could have attempted a double major, or even a triple major, but even then I would have had to cross off some options from my list. Eventually, I chose to enter the world of education. I graduated alongside friends who were business majors, engineering majors, and ministry majors, and though we all left college and found jobs somewhere else, I still knew that my primary goal was to serve God—no matter what my major had been or my current job was. I knew that all work is sacred. It doesn't matter if you are a pastor or priest, or if you work on Wall Street or save lives in a hospital—there is no difference between what we sometimes call the "sacred" and the secular. And it's equally true that no *one person* could do all the things I wanted to do, so I learned to be content and to maximize the path God had given me.

Fast-forward several decades, and God has now placed me in my current role as the president of Grand Canyon University in Phoenix, Arizona. When I arrived at the university, I imme-diately noticed that it was located in a struggling neighborhood overwhelmed with crime, financial hardship, and a lack of resources. Our team wanted to create a world-class university, but we also wanted to lift up and revitalize what had once been a strong, proud, middle-class neighborhood. In 2015 we created a comprehensive and ambitious five-point plan to transform this West Phoenix neighborhood through several public-private partnerships and initiatives. We committed to creating more jobs on campus. We launched businesses that would provide additional jobs for the surrounding community. We collaborated with city leaders to help make our neighborhoods safer. We partnered with Habitat for Humanity to renovate homes in our surrounding community. We worked with public and private K–12 schools to improve the educational opportunities for our neighbors. On my own, I would have hardly made a dent in solving any of these problems. But because we've worked together, as a community, the progress has been transformational.

Another highlight of our progress has been a partnership with a collaborative network of faith-based nonprofits and corporate, retail, and farm and food suppliers through an organization called CityServe. This organization saw that large retailers often have an overabundance of products, so we committed to create a thirty-five-thousand-square-foot warehouse on campus to house these extra products such as clothing, heaters, fans, blankets, furniture, mattresses, food boxes, and other essential items. There are many needs in our neighborhood, throughout the greater Phoenix area, and across Arizona. We want to assist in meeting these needs not only by providing essential household goods to families, but once we get to know the families, we hope to take that relationship even further by providing them with long-term assistance through our nine colleges. We can provide help with job readiness preparation, tutoring, fiscal literacy, addiction counseling, health clinics, and business development. Our hope is to completely change the trajectory these families are currently on and put them on a new path toward prosperity. As I reflect on what we've accomplished so far, I can see how God has used many of my previous decisions to focus my God-given skill and interests, enabling me to contribute to something much greater than I alone could ever have imagined.

My role as university president gives me a unique position to observe how individuals can collaborate together in powerful ways for God's glory. Yet several years ago, something happened that powerfully reminded me of my *own* personal limits. At the time, my two sons were ages nine and eleven, and I was asked to give a talk at a local resort. I brought my sons with me and told them to relax and enjoy themselves in one of the rooms while I was giving my talk. When I finished, I returned to the room, but my sons were nowhere to be found. Immediately concerned, I urged hotel staff and others to help me search for them. After several frantic minutes, I discovered they had left the room and had fallen asleep on lounge chairs next to the pool. It took me three days after that incident to finally calm down! As I later reflected on that moment, I realized that regardless of my skill as a speaker or my competence as a father, it was impossible for me to *both* deliver my talk and watch my kids at the same time. I could not give myself fully to both tasks simultaneously—I was limited in what I could do, even though both were good things.

This gets at just one of the things I like about Dr. McGever's book. In these pages, he explains how God has wisely made every person full of amazing potential—yet also *intentionally* limited. There are limits we innately possess, limits that cannot be exceeded no matter how hard we try because they are limits set by God, not by us. Yet Sean doesn't just leave with that observation, as helpful as it is. He also shows us how God puts us in communities and empowers Christians with the Holy Spirit to exceed our individual limits and accomplish far more than what we can do on our own. I have seen how this is true in my own walk with Christ and in my professional life. Sean shows us how we can move beyond the frustration we often feel in recognizing the reality of our limitations by embracing them and seeing them as a gift.

I met Sean in 2010 in the early days of my tenure at Grand Canyon University, and I invited him to teach for us. Since that time he has excelled as an instructor. His classes quickly fill up with students eager to take them. And during these years of teaching, he has acquired a second masters degree in theology as well as a PhD—all while ministering full time to teenagers in his local community. I mention this because even though this book teaches us about our limits, that doesn't mean those limits minimize what we can achieve. Sean's accomplishments are evidence of this truth.

Looking back, I see that when I declared my undergraduate major many years ago, I thought very carefully about how God had uniquely equipped me for his kingdom. Little did I know that my "limiting" decision—narrowing my options to just one major—would become "good news" to me and a blessing to many others later in my life. As you read this book, I hope Sean's insights and God's Spirit working in your life will accomplish something similar for you.

Brian Mueller
President, Grand Canyon University

ACKNOWLEDGMENTS

I know without a doubt that I am limited. The gracious and wise people below have been on the short end of my limitations and have collaborated with me to do more than I could ever do on my own, by the grace of God—all of this has been *good news* to me.

Thank you to the person who knows my limits better than anyone else—my wife and high school sweetheart, Erin. Thank you also to our children, Caleb, Lilly, and Molly. Each of you are unique, and it is a joy to see how God has brought us all together to bring out the best in each other.

I would also like to thank several friends for helping me to form my ideas in the early stages of this book: Andrew Marin through many conferences, chats on the phone, and rounds of golf; Tremper Longman III, with his sage life and academic advice; Madison Trammel, who saw a spark in my idea early on; and an unnamed dear friend who gave me the idea for this book's title while I was sitting in my local Costco parking lot—you, my friend, are an idea machine. The team at Zondervan, especially Ryan Pazdur, Joshua Kessler, and Kim Tanner, helped me form and polish my ideas beyond anything I could do on my own.

I am grateful for a memorable conversation at a conference

at Durham University, England, with my PhD supervisor, professor Tom Greggs, when he told me that humans have more in common with a head of lettuce than with God. That might sound strange, but it is absolutely true and helpful, as I hope this book will show.

I want to express my gratitude to two sets of students who reversed their roles and taught me. First, my honors Christian Worldview and Systematic Theology 2 classes of Spring 2021 provided fantastic feedback as I shared some of the ideas in this book with them in the midst of a very limiting time in the world. Second, thank you to the three decades of students at Pinnacle High School, with whom I attempted to share the best news ever. I didn't get to tell everyone, but I did the best I could. I've learned to leave the results to God.

> As the heavens are higher than the earth,
> so are my ways higher than your ways
> and my thoughts than your thoughts.
> —Isaiah 55:9

CHAPTER 1

NO LIMITS?

One weekend night last year, in Sky Crossing—an empty, new subdivision under construction—it happened. I unbuckled my seat belt and opened the driver's side door. Stepping out of my car, I walked around to the passenger seat. My son, Caleb, shifted over from the passenger seat, sitting in the driver's seat for the first time. And I taught him how to drive.

After buckling in and checking the mirrors and his surroundings, Caleb pressed the brake pedal and shifted from Park to Drive. He slowly released the brake pedal and moved his foot over to the gas pedal.

That night he encountered many new things. Curbs. Stop signs. Crosswalks. Thankfully, no one was hurt. He did great. I did okay.

The largest indicator on our 2013 Honda Odyssey dashboard relates to the sign Caleb most frequently encountered on his brief inaugural drive: speed. The speedometer indicated how fast he drove, while the sign told him the speed limit. And one of his first (of many) tasks in learning how to drive was remembering to keep an eye on the speed limit while adjusting the speed of our minivan.

After Caleb finished his first driving lesson, he asked me a question—one I didn't know how to answer. "Hey, Dad," he said, "so how fast *can* this Honda Odyssey go?" We looked at the speedometer together and saw that the gauge maxes out at 120 miles per hour. I didn't believe it was possible for our little Odyssey to travel that fast, so we did what most people do when looking for an answer. We looked it up on my phone. It turns out the top speed of a 2013 Honda Odyssey is 117 miles per hour. My son then asked the next obvious question: "Dad, have you ever gone 117 miles per hour in this minivan?" I answered truthfully, saying no, then added, "And I don't think anyone ever should. Besides, the maximum speed limit in our state is seventy-five miles per hour."

Today, Caleb has his driver's license, and he hasn't maxed out our Odyssey—as far as I know.

Roads have speed limits. They have been established by lawmakers. And those limits are good. The engineers at Honda designed the fantastic 2013 Honda Odyssey with limits too. Those limits are good.

You have limits. Everyone has limits. Have you ever wondered what *your* limits are? Have you ever been "pushed to your limits"? Have you pushed other people to theirs?

This book is about the good news of our limits. I hope to show you why we have limits and why they are *good*. We'll look at why we must operate within the bounds of our limits and not just try to expand them endlessly. By the end, I hope to convince you that you should *embrace* your limits. I'll take it one step further and *beg* you to accept your humanity—for your health and your sanity and as a sign of your trust in God.

So let's begin with a question: Did you get everything done last week?

Don't think too hard because I already know your answer. I have the same answer: no.

That's because you are limited. We all are. And believe it or not, this is good news. But how can human limits be *good* news? We'll begin with the claim that God designed human beings as intentionally limited creatures. That statement might land with you in a few ways. It may have even offended some of you. Some might respond, "You don't know me. I hustle and hustle *hard*. Sean, you are providing excuses to lazy people." Others might agree: "Oh, trust me, I know. My life is nothing but a constant catch-up game, trying to keep the spinning plates from falling." Yet another voice might chime in: "I see what you're doing. I accept that I can't do it all, but I won't let you snuff out the dreams God and I have for my life. I am called to dream big. Your claim lacks faith and vision."

Plenty of resources exist to teach you how to maximize your human capacity. The underlying message of these books, seminars, products, apps, and communities is that you can always do more. But can you?

Few people stop and dwell on this question: *Can* I do more? What if a human can't do more? What if there is a limit? And what if that limit was set by God? I write from a distinctly Christian perspective, but this limit applies equally to theists, atheists, agnostics, and everyone in between. The reality of our human limits is obvious, provable, and common, yet repeatedly ignored.

In our society, "hustle culture" coaches people to outwork anyone and everyone around them. On the other side of the hustle spectrum are mindfulness apps and mind-body experiences to guide people to slow down and attempt to pause their reality. Nothing is inherently wrong with hustling or working hard—Scripture encourages a healthy work ethic. Nothing is inherently wrong with slowing down and pausing—the Bible stresses our need to rest. Within God's ordained limits, both ends of this spectrum can be helpful and corrective. But our assumptions about what it means to be human will dictate how we engage the hustle-pause spectrum. It's time to say to the hustle coach, "This is too much. This is beyond my God-given limits." And it's time to say to the relaxation center staff, "I cannot transcend my existence. This is beyond my God-given limits." And for most of us, embracing the good news of our limits sounds more like this: "I cannot join the PTA / sign up for this Bible study / read this book / volunteer for that task / try to meet or help more people / learn more about that topic / travel to that place . . . I want to say yes, but I *have* to say no."

There are three key reasons why we have limits and why those limits are good. But first let me tell you a story.

THE MILE

I started running for exercise this year because my daughter Lilly joined her high school cross-country team. When I stepped out the door for my first run, I couldn't remember the last time I had done this. And I certainly had no sense of my running pace. To make the process of running a little more fun,

I downloaded a running app and pressed Start. As I labored with each stride, I felt like my tendons were going to explode off my legs. And that was only three minutes into my light jog. I constantly looked down at the app to check my pace. And after finishing my short run—interspersed with a few much-needed walks—I delved into the data. Honest confession: I love stats. I quickly learned that my first mile was eleven minutes. My second mile was *much* slower.

That first run was pretty rough. Still, I kept at it and began to enjoy running more than I thought I would. As crazy as it might sound, the stats helped hook me. During every run, and immediately after, I would review my data (I still do). The two numbers I look at are the total mileage and the pace for each mile. By studying these, I've discovered my running limits. I hope to get faster and run farther, of course, but I've also come to realize that no matter how hard I train, there is a limit to what I can do as a runner.

Richard Webster of England set the men's world record for the mile in the year 1865. His time was four minutes, thirty-six seconds. Roger Bannister finally broke the notorious four-minute mile barrier on May 6, 1954, in Oxford, England. His record lasted forty-six days. When I looked up the current record (as of this writing), it is an amazing three minutes, forty-three seconds, set by Hicham El Guerrouj of Morocco while running in Rome in 1999. We can see that from 1865 to 1999, the fastest mile improved by almost a minute.

So is three minutes, forty-three seconds the fastest possible mile time? Has El Guerrouj established the limit for the fastest mile a human can run? Probably not. If the record mile decreased by almost a minute over the course of about 135 years, will the new record be about a minute faster 135 years from now? Will a human being run a mile in under three minutes in 2150? Maybe. Will someone run a mile in under two minutes? One minute? Thirty seconds? One second? Half a second?

I know I am pushing this scenario to the point of being ridiculous. Maybe you, or a snarky friend, would answer me by suggesting time travel or teleportation from one place to another like in the old *Star Trek* TV show. Fair enough. But I'm asking about the serious possibility of another human running a mile *under the same conditions* as Richard Webster did in 1865 and Hicham El Guerrouj did in 1999. Is that same task of running one mile humanly possible in one second? No. And it never will be. That task, that goal, is well beyond the limit of natural human capacities.

THE RUGBY MATCH, THE FEIS, AND THE MEET

My wife and I have three teenage children. Five years ago, all three of them played on the North Valley Scorpions rugby team. One of the best parts of that season was that most of their practices and games were on the same days, at the same times, and at the same locations. So on any given Saturday, we would load up our beloved Costco-bought trailer full of chairs, bottles of water, sunscreen (the Arizona sun always wins), and snacks and hunker down near the rugby field for a few hours. Our kids had other activities they were involved in that year, but rugby, and its coordinated scheduling, was the glue that held our family calendar together.

This year our schedule looks different. My son still plays

rugby. But my two daughters—and, yes, they both enjoyed playing rugby for several years—have moved on to focus on other activities.

Earlier this year we had a Saturday when my wife was at my daughter's Irish dance feis competition (pronounced "fesh," in case you're interested), I was at my son's rugby match, and our other daughter was attending a cross-country meet. For some of you reading this, this situation is not too hard to imagine. Your activities are likely different (any fellow rugby, Irish dance, cross-country families out there?), but the scenario is common for many families with children involved in multiple activities. Life is busy. Full.

The math behind these circumstances is easy to calculate. Two parents + three kids + three activities = *we can't be at everything.* There is no way to solve this difficult parental and relational situation. And even when the math *could* work and we can each attend an event, life tends to complicate our schedule.

We can't be at everything. I can't turn into two people for the sake of my children's events, no matter how much I might want to. One of the limitations of being human is that I can be in only one place at a time, and there is no way around this. It is one of the limits that defines us.

JEOPARDY!

The *Jeopardy!* theme song causes my heart to beat with excitement. Whenever I answer a question correctly, I feel smart. And when I get a question wrong or don't know the answer, well, I don't feel all that bad. For me, the show is pretty much all upside and very little downside, with a few commercials and awkward contestant interviews mixed in.

My family recently binged past seasons of *Jeopardy!* Our kids are a bit older now, so they can appreciate the game, and the nationwide lockdown gave us some extra time together. For those who haven't seen it, *Jeopardy!* is a trivia game. The more you know, the better you will do. When my kids were in elementary school, they didn't know as much. So, for example, recent *Jeopardy!* topics such as Words in September, Name the Automaker, At the Movies, or -logies would have stumped them. But now my children know more, and I guess you could say they know *just enough* information to enjoy the game. They have sufficient knowledge to participate at the lowest threshold of *Jeopardy!* enthusiasts.

My family also enjoys the quirks and personalities of both the winners and the losers. One of the most exciting parts of the show is when someone for whom we are rooting wins the game and then comes back in the next episode and wins again. After watching for a few weeks, my family wanted to know who was the most successful *Jeopardy!* contestant ever?

There is a bit of a debate about how to best judge who has been the most successful player on *Jeopardy!* Brad Rutter won the most money: over $4.6 million. Most of this came through winning several "tournaments of champions" hosted intermittently over fourteen years. Ken Jennings holds the longest winning streak, in which he won over $2.5 million over a seventy-four-game run in 2004. James Holzhauer, a professional gambler from Las Vegas, was the fastest contestant to win $1 million. He finished with over $2.4 million dollars in a thirty-two-game winning streak. He famously bet all his money on every Daily Double.

My kids are on one end of the *Jeopardy!* spectrum, and on the other end are Brad Rutter, Ken Jennings, and James Holzhauer. "What is this spectrum?" you might ask. It is the spectrum of *Jeopardy!*-relevant information—what some might consider "trivia," or trivial, nonessential information. But let's assume for the moment that we are talking about information in general, not only the facts and trivia you'd need to win *Jeopardy!* In that, my kids would have some advantages on certain topics. For example, my kids know a lot more than Ken Jennings does about our local youth rugby club.

One of my favorite things about *Jeopardy!* is that sometimes an "answer" is given and none of the contestants know the "question" (which is how you win). There were times when Brad, Ken, and James were silent because they did not know enough information to answer. When that happens, we viewers feel just a little more human. We are reminded that we cannot know everything there is to know, even in the limited domain of *Jeopardy!*-relevant information. Knowing everything falls well beyond the limit of human capacity.

And again, we are confronted by this reality: You have limits. I have limits. Ken Jennings has limits. We all do. Running the mile, choosing what events to attend, and playing *Jeopardy!* prove to us that we all have inherent limitations. Running the mile shows us we don't have the capacity or power to do whatever we want. Our capacity and power are limited. Having to choose which event to attend shows us we don't have the capacity to be present whenever and wherever we want. Our presence is limited. And playing *Jeopardy!* and watching even the "champions" play *Jeopardy!*—and occasionally miss an answer—tells us that no one can "know it all." Our capacity for knowledge and information is inherently limited.

These are simple, everyday realities. Everyone knows we have limits, and some of them are more obvious than others. The problem, as we will see in the coming chapters, is that we are easily tricked into thinking we have no limits. Worse, we are made to feel we are inadequate when we fall short of humanly unattainable limits.

CHRISTIAN "LIMITS"

There is a sneaky, devious, and—I dare say—evil distortion that tells us that our human limitations are "bad" or wrong. Sadly, these messages come from a surprising group of people: Christians. I don't presume to know the motives behind those who promote these messages. Yet these messages are dangerous, unhealthy, and untrue. Most of the time they are a call to walk in faith and meant to encourage risk-taking. They grow from promises that we can do all things, that nothing is impossible, and that if we trust God, we will be able to do what we never could otherwise. While these promises are true, this type of thinking is a deceptive lie that encourages us to think our created limitations are wrong. It confuses our sinful lack of faith in God with our God-given, created limitations.

The most easily identifiable of these Christian messages comes from an isolated and out-of-context Bible verse: Philippians 4:13. It's usually shortened to something like, "I can do all things." I just typed the phrase *I can do all things* into Amazon's search bar, and I found products with that phrase in twenty-eight Amazon departments. If you need something inspirational for your dog, you can buy the "I Can Do All Things

Pet Cute Clothes" for $12.99. Parents can buy a linen poster of Oscar the Grouch with this message printed on it for a nursery room for only $6.95. You go, Oscar! If you are a garlic lover and have $17.94, you can order three hundred "delicious smooth and creamy butter mints" with wrapping that reminds you "I can do all things through Christ."

Boxing fans might remember former heavyweight champion Evander "The Real Deal" Holyfield, who walked into his fight with Mike Tyson with "Phil. 4:13" printed on his robe and shorts. Perhaps Holyfield embraced the true message of this verse, which is to be content with who you are and what God has given you, no matter the outcome or circumstances. But most people probably understood Holyfield's message as a belief that he expected to win his boxing match by God's power.

Or maybe you are more familiar with two-time NBA MVP and three-time NBA champion Stephen Curry. Don't get me wrong, I'm not here to hate on Steph. In fact, I'm a big fan. Steph Curry also adopted the phrase *I can do all things* as his personal motto and marketing moniker. The athletic company Under Armour even has a line of apparel associated with Curry, and this phrase on it. Oddly enough, in 2017, Under Armour received a cease and desist demand from another apparel company claiming trademark infringement. Last I checked, the legal process hasn't finished. Apparently, you *can't* do all things, not even when you are just *saying* you can do all things—at least not without possibly breaking the law.

In fairness, many Christians are aware of the misuse of Philippians 4:13 and tend to give well-intentioned believers the benefit of the doubt. Steph, don't hate me; Evander, don't beat me up.

This all-too-common tendency is ultimately rooted in a *wrong understanding of Jesus and of ourselves*. As we will learn, all of us—including many Christians—look at the life of Jesus Christ, and we assume we are meant to be his equal in every way. Jesus Christ is human and we are human, so we should strive to be like Jesus, right?

But this (false) Christian logic neglects an important difference. While Jesus was fully human, he was also uniquely God. And even though we should seek to be like Jesus, that does not mean we become like God in every way. In some ways we become like God, but in many other ways we remain subject to God's created limitations. The faulty logic works like this:

God has no limits.
Jesus is God.
Jesus has no limits.
Jesus is human.
I am human.
I have no limits (through Christ).

This line of thinking tempts us not to think twice when we read, "I can do all things through Christ," and to assume this statement means that as Christians our human limits have been expanded or redefined. But this assumption ignores a key difference between Jesus, who has two natures, and you and me. We don't *become* God. We remain human, with all our created limitations, and learn to follow Jesus by faith, walking in the power of God's Holy Spirit. Grasping this difference is one of the keys to embracing our God-given limits as *good* limits.

Many of the popular messages we hear today, both inside

and outside the church, urge us to push further, dig deeper, break through barriers, and dream bigger. Some of us need to hear a word of encouragement. We've tried and failed, or we've lost faith. Our vision has grown narrow and small. And we need to be stretched and pushed to become all we can be within our God-given limitations.

But others of us take these messages too far. In embracing the call to dream big and walk by faith, we ignore the biblical truth that our Creator intentionally made us *with limits*, and he declared this to be good. We recall from Genesis that God made all creation, including humans, "very good" (Gen. 1:31). To put it bluntly, the fact that I will never run a one-minute mile, be able to attend all the events I want to attend, or know the answers to every *Jeopardy!* question is something *God intended, a feature of how he created us.* When God made you, the God of the universe declared that everything that you are, *including your limitations,* is "very good."

GUILT AT HIGH SCHOOL GRADUATIONS

So why does any of this matter? Why write an entire book about this topic? In short, I don't want you to go through what I've gone through. I want to save you from the pain of going down the wrong road.

I'm an "achiever." I work hard and give it my all. But I also fail miserably, and I'm not just talking about making mistakes, though I make plenty of those too. I do everything I can to maximize what I'm capable of doing, seeking to be as productive and efficient as I can be—and yet still feel like I'm not doing, being, or achieving enough. Even when I have my best days and then imagine linking those days together into my best week and even into a full year, I'm still short of my "best." I'm forced to accept that my best is always inherently limited. And the truth is that I'm rarely, if ever, at my best.

This book isn't about me. Like anyone, I have my own issues, beliefs, and experiences; each one of us is a multilayered, complex individual. Your story is not the same as mine; we all have different gifts, strengths, and staminas. Yet we are all the same in one important regard—we are all human. And because of that, each one of us inevitably feels guilty when our accomplishments don't align with our false beliefs about what we are humanly capable of doing, when we believe we can fulfill expectations that don't reflect (or accept) reality.

I have worked with teenagers for over twenty years. Prior to my junior year of high school, I rarely went to church and did not consider myself religious. My friends and a youth leader invited me to some events, and a few months later, Jesus Christ changed my life and altered my path. Since 1994 I have reached out to teenagers with the hope that they too might encounter and follow Christ. I consider myself a missionary to our local high school, hoping to reach young people who are as I once was.

An unavoidable dynamic of working with high school students is that our relationships are cyclical. Each year, a new class of freshmen enter high school, and the seniors depart as they graduate. Familiar people leave and new people arrive. This cycle repeats year after year. Each August, our local high school begins with "freshman camp." Each May, the school rents out a small local baseball stadium for graduation.

Frequently, the school asks me to help with some of the

freshman camps. The students are lost, confused, and not sure who to talk to. As they spill through the doors, I am often overwhelmed by all the new faces. After they are seated, I look up and see eight hundred students sitting in the bleachers. I scan the crowd, row by row, silently praying that God will work in their lives, if not today, then hopefully soon. As the event progresses, students begin to loosen up. They are welcomed. Schedules are handed out. Tours are given. School clubs are announced. Pizza is served. And the following week, each August, school begins.

Three and a half years later, each May, a similar process repeats at graduation. Students spill through the doors onto a field. They find their seats. They are a little less lost and confused, and now they know who to talk to. I always attend. I grab a program and find my seat. Graduations are long events, especially when there are several hundred graduates, but the length gives me time to look over all the names in the program.

My first pass through the names in the program is a fun one. "There he is! Oh, look at that one! I'm so glad he made it." Looking over the names reveals a dozen or so that bring to mind old memories and reminders of meaningful conversations and experiences together. By the time I am done with my first pass, the staff have begun reading the names of the students whose last names begin with *B*. I settle further into my seat and look through the names again. Several dozen new names grab my attention. I think, "Wow, I haven't heard from him in a while. Oh, yikes, I could have done a better job showing up to his baseball games. Oh, there's the girl I met at the freshman camp years ago; I haven't talked to her since then." By then we are usually at the *C*s and *D*s. And that's when it always hits me. There are several hundred students I have *never* seen, heard of, talked to, or even known they existed. Out of the eight hundred graduates, I usually know around a dozen well. There are several dozen more I tried to connect with. In some cases I attempted to reach out and flat out *failed* to impact their lives. And there is the vast majority that simply walked past me on campus for four years.

High school graduations are an annual guilt trip.

After the ceremony finishes, I'll grab a few fun photos with the graduates and then walk back to my car. I feel about 5 percent successful, 95 percent a failure, and 100 percent hoping to do better the next year. As I buckle my seat belt and start my car, the thoughts race through my head: "I wasn't enough, I couldn't do what I wanted to do, and I once again crashed into the hard, brick wall of my limits."

Two years ago, though, I had an epiphany—a vision. God gave me clarity about how to better understand myself, my calling, my community, and my God. He taught me that we all have limitations, and we can't take a shortcut or detour around them.

I simply can't do everything I want to do.

A restaurant down the street from my house has a massive menu. It has everything you could ever want to eat. I went there once and never went back. The pizza was slimy. The egg rolls were mushy. The soup was watery. The meatloaf was burnt from being untouched too long under the heat lamps. The fish was . . . well, just don't eat the fish. I have no idea why it is still open. It is always virtually empty. Judging on how often they fail to replace the fluorescent lights on their street sign, I'm guessing profits are scarce. It clearly struggles to stay open. A massive selection of mediocrity has not helped them succeed. Nearby is a simple pizza place, and it is always packed. They now have dozens of locations in our state. They have two basic items on their menu: great pizza and great salad—that's it.

Many of us today are tempted to do it all, to be everything, to do the impossible. But I want you to consider being like a great pizza place. Don't be a terrible buffet of mediocre food. Embrace who God has made you to be, and then, within your God-given limits, be the person he made you to be. You may not be a world-class athlete or the next tech billionaire. You may not be everything you hope to be or do all you want to do. But God is asking you to do only what you can with whatever he has given you. And rather than wasting time trying to do things he has not asked or empowered you to do, try spending more time and energy focused on the gifts and abilities he *has* given you.

Believe me, that we have limits is good news. But before we learn *how* to embrace our limitations, we must confront the pernicious lie that we can do anything we want if we simply try (or hustle) harder. That's a recipe for disaster . . . but why?

CHAPTER 2

HUMANS ARE *LIKE GOD?*

When my children were younger, they loved dressing up. It didn't matter what day of the year it was; every day was dress-up day. The aisles of the grocery store, Target, and Home Depot were filled with the click-clack of hard plastic princess shoes and worn-out children's cowboy boots. One of the best gifts my son ever received was called My Superhero Starter Kit. The packaging described it as "super simple crafting with little to no parental involvement." That checked all the boxes for me. "Have at it," I said to my son. Hours later, my son emerged from his room to introduce us to his alter ego. He came around the corner as The Fantastic Lightning!

Let me tell you about The Fantastic Lightning. Inside his "power cuffs" was where he "kept his powers." That's logical. Of course you need to keep your powers in your *power* cuffs! Where else would you keep them? His mask had lightning bolts on it to zap the bad guys. His cape allowed him to "fly faster than a speeding bullet." As if that weren't enough for a superhero, he told us he would save the world through the power of the four green bullets from his Nerf gun. To stay fleet-footed, he stepped into his fluffy, yellow duck slippers. The world had found its lowercase-*S* savior!

The key objective for The Fantastic Lightning, after saving the world, was to "shoot bad guys small," by which he meant he made bad guys really tiny. How tiny? He would show us by holding his fingers up to his face, as if holding up tweezers to his eye, and say, "This small." Bad people beware—it is tough to be bad when you're the size of a yellow Lego head. One of my daughters got in on the action as well. She created her own superhero outfit, no starter kit needed. Her signature superpower was to get bad guys by shooting flowers at them.

I didn't have to encourage my kids' desire to be superheroes. They caught the idea everywhere they looked in stories, shows, and the movies we enjoyed. When I last checked, the Marvel Cinematic Universe was the highest-grossing movie franchise of all time, netting over $22.5 billion. The dream of possessing superhuman powers has proven quite profitable. We are all excited by the idea of exceeding our human limitations with powers that take us beyond what is typical or ordinary.

SUPERHUMANS, LETTUCE, AND DOGS

We know from personal experience what it is like to be human. But we dream and wonder, "What would it be like to be superhuman?" This curiosity has crept into the Christian imagination through a surprising window. Many believers read the Bible's stories about Jesus doing supernatural works and empowering others to do these works. And so we wonder, "Is this possible for me too?"

When I was in college, my friends invited me to join them on weekends at a few meeting rooms in some B-level hotels on the edge of town. The gatherings looked similar to a church service, but they were distinctively different. The organizers had structured the meetings to highlight the leader of the group, who claimed to have miraculous gifts of healing and prophecy. In those days, miraculous gifts were a controversial topic, and even today they remain so in some circles. My point is not to debate the veracity or continuation of the sign gifts; I simply want to highlight the frenetic curiosity and zeal my friends had for this individual. They thought they a real-life superhuman, someone who could do the impossible, who fit the mold of what they had read in their Bibles. Incidentally, the meetings these leaders held would rarely last more than a few months.

I raise the topic of miraculous gifts to highlight our desire to see someone who does the impossible, who seems to exceed the normal, everyday limits of human existence. The reality is that Christians don't have superpowers. We have the exact same *human* capacities as our non-Christian neighbors. We have the same created limitations as well. Yes, we have the empowerment of the Holy Spirit, which we will discuss carefully in a later chapter of this book. But even when we talk of God empowering human beings, we aren't speaking of a change in who we are or how we are made.

My doctoral supervisor frequently liked to remind me that we, as human beings, have more in common with a head of lettuce than with the God of the universe. The first time I heard him say that, I was confused and offended. How dare he compare me to arugula! But after giving it some thought, I realized that his statement held an important truth. There is a fundamental difference between the Creator and the stuff he creates. Lettuce is a created thing. And human beings are created as well. You and I are both created beings. Though I have a few things going for me that a head of lettuce might envy, we are still in that same broad category: we are created things.

A repeated metaphor in the Bible describes God as the potter and humans as the clay.

> Remember that you molded me like clay.
>> Will you now turn me to dust again? (Job 10:9)

> I am the same as you in God's sight;
>> I too am a piece of clay. (Job 33:6)

> Does the clay say to the potter,
>> "What are you making?" (Isa. 45:9)

> Yet you, LORD, are our Father.
>> We are the clay, you are the potter;
>> we are all the work of your hand. (Isa. 64:8)

> Like clay in the hand of the potter, so are you in my hand, Israel. (Jer. 18:6)

I was reminded of this relationship—between the potter and his clay—after finding myself with a dog this last year. For the first forty-two years of my life, I never owned a dog, nor did I imagine I would *ever* have a dog. But children are persistent. More precisely, my daughters are persistent, and eventually they won that battle. Euan, our dog, entered our home a little over a year ago. I have learned not to expect too much or too little of him. As much as I try, I can't get Euan to play fetch. That might happen one day, but it is looking more and more unlikely. The other night, we were watching *Jeopardy!* (again). Euan did not bark out any correct answers. Euan's capacities appear to be pretty limited. I have learned, however, not to underestimate what Euan *can* do. He learned quickly what the words *treat, walk,* and *food* mean. Good friends of mine had told me that dogs can have great capacity for loyalty and perceiving our emotions, and now I know they were right.

Why do I bring up my dog, Euan? Because Euan and I have more in common than God and I do. I am more like a dog than God is like me.

We know from the first phrase of the Bible that God created the heavens and the earth. No human, no dog, no head of lettuce can do that. I have never willed anything from nonexistence to existence. At best, I have altered, or remolded, existing material into something else, but I never made matter appear out of nothing.

God tells Adam in Genesis 2:17 not to eat from the tree of the knowledge of good and evil. In the following chapter, Satan tempts Adam and Eve to eat from this tree and explains, "When you eat from it your eyes will be opened, and you will be like God, knowing good and evil" (Gen. 3:5). The desire for an additional capacity (that is, to know good from evil), a capacity that would supposedly make them more like God, was a sufficiently tempting desire. We know how they responded. They ate.

God made the distinction between creator and creation, potter and clay, God and humans, God and "gods" clear in the commandments:

> You shall have no other gods before me.
> You shall not make for yourself an image in the form
>   of anything in heaven above or on the earth
>   beneath or in the waters below. You shall not bow
>   down to them or worship them. (Ex. 20:3–5)

None of us should be in the practice of forming things to worship. Clay should not attempt to make potters. Yet when Moses came down from Mount Sinai, the people were doing exactly that.

The clay wants to be the potter. Humans want more than our original design allows. This happened in the garden of Eden, and it still happens today.

The Old Testament is filled with warnings to "stay in our lane" as human beings, created by God. Yes, the Old Testament has many examples of people performing superhuman feats. Moses, Elijah, Elisha, Isaiah, and Daniel experienced and announced supernatural works firsthand. Yet none of them claimed that the power for these works came from them. No, the power always came from God, even when he used people in the process. Consider Daniel's explanation of what happened to him in the lions' den, when he was saved from being eaten: "My God sent his angel, and he shut the mouths of the lions" (Dan. 6:22). Isaiah explained the miracle of the sun's shadow going backward and not forward by saying, "The LORD made the shadow go back" (2 Kings 20:11). The prophets made their requests and predicted God's mighty plans. They were capable of *asking* and *announcing*, but they themselves could not *do* these supernatural, superhuman works.

JESUS CHRIST: PROBLEM PERSON?

The Old Testament delivers clear examples of those who were able to do superhuman, miraculous feats *through* God's power. But it never mistakes a prophet or a miracle worker for God. God and human beings are in two distinct categories. The New Testament, however, presents us with something new. It presents us with a person who breaks the pattern, a man who does not clearly separate human and divine capacities. He doesn't "stay in his lane" as a human. This "problem" person is Jesus Christ.

Jesus experienced a fully human life. Jesus was tempted (Matt. 4:1), got hungry (Matt. 4:2), was thirsty (John 19:28), grew tired (John 4:6), slept (Matt. 8:24), cried (John 11:35; Luke 19:41), bled (John 19:34), loved others (Mark 10:21), and felt compassion (Matt. 9:36). Jesus was conceived supernaturally (more on that later), but he had a normal human birth (Luke 2:7) and grew just as others did (Luke 2:52). Like other humans, Jesus had a physical body (Matt. 8:3) and an immaterial spirit (Mark 2:8). The author of Hebrews wrote, "For this reason he had to be made like them, fully human in every way, in order that he might become a merciful and faithful high priest in service to God, and that he might make atonement for the sins of the people. Because he himself suffered when he was tempted, he is able to help those who are being tempted" (Heb. 2:17–18).

Jesus was made "fully human in every way," saving us through his atonement. And now he is able to help us when we are tempted.

Some people throughout history have questioned the full humanity of Jesus. Usually, these questions arose because they struggled to understand how a transcendent God could come into a finite material world and still remain God.

The earliest followers of Jesus never doubted that he was a human being. And through the centuries, Christians have always believed that Jesus is fully human. But here is where the problem arises. People worship Jesus, yet he is fully human. And the Old Testament clearly taught us that we shouldn't worship *any created thing or person*, and that includes other humans. So how is it that the early Christians—and the church for over two thousand years—are okay with worshiping another human, specifically Jesus of Nazareth, the Jewish Messiah.

Some might argue, "Yes, but that's after he resurrected. That's when they started worshiping him." Yet the Bible is clear that even from his birth, people worshiped Jesus. They worshiped an infant. Yes, a little, crying, snorting, hungry, dependent, baby boy who peed and pooped. Matthew records that when the magi found baby Jesus, "they bowed down and worshiped him" (Matt. 2:11). We don't know a lot about the magi, and we don't know if they fully adhered to the beliefs and teaching of the Old Testament. Regardless, bowing down and worshiping a baby is certainly odd, yet it foreshadowed what was to come.

From the beginning of his ministry, Jesus reiterated the Old Testament teaching that it was improper to worship anyone other than God. In his forty-day wilderness temptation, Jesus reminded Satan that the Scripture instructs us to "worship the Lord your God, and serve him only" (Matt. 4:10).

■ ■ ■

An overlooked graphics format that most people don't know a lot about—even though they use it all the time—is called ICO. When computers transitioned from MS-DOS to "Windows-style" desktops, they began using an ICO graphics file, which stood for an "icon" file. This file was a small picture that the user recognized and associated with the computer program the user wanted to launch. You are familiar with icon files whether you know it or not.

We also encounter icons in another context. Many of these originated as brands, logos, or trademarks, but they function much the same. Think Nike's swoosh. Apple's apple. Twitter's bird. Instagram's camera outline. They are visual images, we can picture them, and we immediately know what they mean or, better, what they represent. A swoosh is not a shoe company, an apple is not a technology giant, and a bird or a camera is not a social media platform. A swoosh, apple, bird, and camera are all icons. The icons we see on our smartphones and computer desktops represent something else. They serve as pointers—whether that is to a computer program we want to run, an app on our smartphone, or a company the image visually represents.

An icon is something that represents something else. But it is *not* the thing itself.

You are an *icon* of God. You were made to remind others of, point to, and give a faint impression of God. Every human being has this capacity, and this is part of what it means when the Bible tells us we are made in the image and likeness of God (Gen. 1:26–27). In the same way that a swoosh makes us think of the company Nike, you and I are meant to make everyone think of God. In the ancient Near East, kings frequently set up statues of themselves throughout their kingdoms to make their presence known. The statues were not the king; the king was the king. But the statues *reminded* everyone that the king was the king. In a similar way, God designed you and me to remind everyone that the King is the King.

The Old Testament was translated from Hebrew to Greek a few centuries before Jesus was born. The Hebrew word in Genesis 1:26 normally translated as "image" is *tselem*. This word was translated into the Greek word *eikōn*, from which we get the English word *icon*. Icons on our phones or computers point to the program. Icons in sports or entertainment point to teams or companies. You are an icon of God because you were made in the image of God. Another place we encounter "icons" are the images in mirrors. When you look directly in a mirror, you see a representation of yourself. If the mirror is clean—not warped, cracked, or broken—you see a clear image of yourself. But the image on the surface of the mirror is not actually you. There aren't two of you. There is only one. You are made in the image of God, but there is only one God.

It was God's intention in the beginning to make human beings his image bearers and for them to be fruitful and multiply, filling the earth with the image and likeness of God. Yet that didn't happen, at least not without a significant interruption. When human beings disobeyed God, his image remained, but it became blurry, making it difficult for others to see fully the goodness of God in his image bearers. Jesus came, in part, to restore our ability to fully display God's likeness to others.

It shouldn't surprise us that we are tempted to worship other human beings (or even ourselves). Paul warned us of this temptation, that sin would call us to worship and serve created things rather than the Creator (Rom. 1:25). We are prone to worship other people because humans are made in the image of God. And when we look at that image, we see a hint of something amazing that we don't see anywhere else in God's creation. When we see even a foggy outline of love, joy, peace, patience, kindness, goodness, faithfulness, gentleness, or self-control, we like what we see. We like it because we see something that looks *like* God, even if the image is blurred and warped. Sadly, human sin distorts, cracks, and all-but-destroys the image of God in us. It remains as evidence of God's grace and reminds us that every person deserves dignity and respect, that human life is special because of our unique task of representing God to one another. Nonetheless, the image does not work the way it was originally intended. And worse, we find this distorted image worth worshiping in place of God. The most idolized objects on earth are our fellow human beings.

JESUS LOOKS IN THE MIRROR AND LIKES WHAT HE SEES

Last week my wife and I drove to Sedona, Arizona, for our wedding anniversary. In Sedona, iron-rich mountains radiate through layers of bare red rock that tower nearly vertically amid winding roads. Everywhere you turn, the landscape is photoworthy. The red rock stuns and overpowers the senses. We found it difficult to know how high or distant the mountains were from us. Sometimes we would get into a conversation and, with a brief glance, look up and be overwhelmed by what surrounded us. It was difficult to soak it all in.

After the sun set, the mountains became shadows, but the

show wasn't over. Sedona is a great place to look at the stars. On our first night, it was as if the Big Dipper jumped out of the sky like a neon sign flashing "Look at me!" With ease, my fingers traced the dipper and bent handle of the familiar shape.

The outline of the Big Dipper was easy to recognize, at least from my perspective. In reality, the seven stars of the Big Dipper are not next to each other as they appear to be. Our eyes don't allow us to have star depth perception. The closest star of the Big Dipper, called Merak, is over 79 light years from earth. Merak is the bottom part of the dipper farthest from the handle. The top part of the dipper directly "above" Merak is the star called Dubhe. Dubhe is the most distant of the Big Dipper stars: 123 light years away from earth. While Merak and Dubhe look like they are right next to each other, they aren't—they are over 44 light years from each other. In other words, when we look up at the Big Dipper, the stars look close together, but if we went in a spaceship off to the side of the Big Dipper, we would realize they are very far from each other—it is all a matter of perspective. We are humanly limited in our perception of reality, but telescopes and other tools astronomers use help us grasp what we are really looking at when we look at stars in the sky.

Jesus was born fully human. He was human just as you and I are human. Yet there was another dynamic to Jesus that not everyone saw. The magi saw it, Mary knew it, and Joseph knew it too. In time, many would come to know it. Jesus is not only fully human, Jesus is also fully divine.

Jesus's humanity was easy to perceive, like recognizing the outline of the Big Dipper on a clear night. People in the first century needed no special insight and hardly any time to conclude, "That Jesus over there—the one people are looking at—he's a human."

But Jesus's divinity wasn't always as easy to perceive. When people listened to his teaching and saw his deeds and miracles, they knew he was a very unusual human, and many came to realize, as Thomas did, that he is also Lord and God (John 20:28).

You are human. Jesus is human. Yet while you are created *in* the image of God (Gen. 1:26), Jesus Christ *is* the image of God (2 Cor. 4:4). It is this image, the image of Jesus Christ, to which we are to be conformed (Rom. 8:29). Jesus Christ is not only the *image*, he is also the *Creator*. Paul wrote, "The Son is the image of the invisible God, the firstborn over all creation. For in him all things were created: things in heaven and on earth, visible and invisible, whether thrones or powers or rulers or authorities; all things have been created through him and for him" (Col. 1:15–16).

When you stand in front of a mirror, there are at least two parts: *you* and the *image* in the mirror. In writing to the Colossians, Paul helped them to understand that Jesus is both the being standing in front of the mirror (the transcendent Creator) and the perfect reflection of that being too. In the same way that astronomers explain to us a fuller perspective of what we are seeing when we look up at the stars, Paul and the rest of the New Testament explain to us a more complete picture of what we are seeing when we look at Jesus Christ. Jesus is fully human and fully God. You and I are *only* fully human.

YOU ARE SO ONE-DIMENSIONAL

When we don't grasp the distinction between Jesus's two natures and our single nature, we are prone to stress ourselves out—and those around us too. When we don't appreciate this difference, we don't understand the good news of our limits. Because, as it turns out, no matter how hard you try, you can't be *exactly* like Jesus, even if you are a Christian.

We often get confused when we look at Christ. Christ's human and divine natures aren't easy to perceive. His natures are a bit like the distance between the stars in the Big Dipper. And so, in some cases, a misreading of the life of Jesus Christ blurs the depth perception of our human limits. You may be quite surprised when we take time later in this book to reread some of the stories in the Gospels. As it turns out, even though Jesus was divine and did feats we can't do (like dying on a cross for the sins of others), the majority of Jesus's life modeled for us *how to live within our human limits.*

For now, everything we have been talking about boils down to one simple but essential truth. I mentioned it briefly in the last chapter. And it might seem so obvious, and in some ways so ridiculous, that you might wonder why I feel the need to bring it up again.

Here is the truth: you are not God.

When someone becomes a Christian, new relationships, even new life, are available to them in a renewed connection with God. (We'll talk more about this in chapters 7 and 8 of this book.) And our sinful human nature is redeemed. But it continues to be human. Christians don't add a divine nature to their human nature.

SUPERMAN AT CAMP

Almost a decade ago, I spoke at a camp for junior high students and their leaders, some of whom were parents. I prayed about my content and chose a fitting theme, which I would cover over the course of five days. I decided to talk about superheroes. For my "hook," I talked about how the Hulk is incredibly powerful, how Iron Man can fly, and how the Avengers are stronger when they work together. My favorite superhero, the one I talked about the first night, is Superman. Superman has many superpowers: superstrength, superspeed, X-ray vision, and, best of all, the ability to fly.

Throughout those five days, I mentioned Superman repeatedly. After each session, the students went back to their cabins to discuss the talk with their leaders, and at the end of the week, we had an all-camp sharing time. Thankfully, God used the talks and the discussions in some exciting ways. Many of the stories the students and leaders shared began with a fun reference to a superhero and then moved on to something far more personal and meaningful.

The last person to share was a father who attended the camp as a leader for his son's group. He first shared about the meaningful time he and his son had at camp. Then he mentioned that he had one additional point to make about superheroes. The stage lights were shining in my face, so I squinted to see better. He looked familiar, but I couldn't quite place him.

"Sean," he said, "that clip you showed from the Superman movie was good, but I would have preferred a clip from the TV series *Lois & Clark: The New Adventures of Superman*. The kids and leaders in the audience all laughed. I was confused, not sure why everyone was laughing, but to avoid looking like an idiot, I laughed along too. We wrapped up the sharing time, thanked everyone for coming, prayed, and told them they were free to leave. A few leaders and kids came up right away to say goodbye before I left. The last person to come up was that father again. As he stepped closer, I once again had the odd feeling that I knew him from somewhere.

Then, all at once, I understood why everyone had laughed earlier. The dad standing before me was none other than Dean Cain, the actor who had played Superman in the *Lois & Clark* TV show, a show I had watched every week as a teenager. I had a brief, fun chat with Dean and his son, and when the room cleared out, it finally dawned on me that I had been speaking about Superman all week long while "Superman" had been right there in the audience. My childhood memories crumbled and reformed in a strange way. Dean had been nice to me all that week, and I was impressed that he, like many other wonderful parents, had taken a week of his time to listen and learn about Jesus alongside his son. But in that moment, my worlds collided, and the Superman I had known from watching television as a child disappeared. I realized he was just as human as everyone else—and always had been, of course.

Maybe you've had that experience too—when your heroes have shown themselves to be simply a regular person.

I was especially vulnerable to this letdown in the first few years after becoming a Christian. Several people made significant investments in my life in those days, and their impact was so influential and powerful that I lifted them up to superhuman status. Calling them my heroes is not a stretch. Yet over time—and it didn't take long—I realized my heroes were not as superhuman as I imagined. They couldn't fix my problems. They didn't spend as much time with me as I had hoped. They came late or left meetings early, or they forgot about meetings altogether. They didn't remember promises they had made to me.

At first I took it personally, as if I were the issue, that I was to blame or was unworthy or had failed them in some way. Then, as I shifted into a bit more jaded perspective, I blamed *them*. "Oh, how the mighty have fallen," I said to myself. When I opened my eyes a bit further, I saw them failing other people too, including their families. Mind you, these were some wonderful people—truly some of the best humans and Christians I have ever met. But the real issue wasn't their failures or mine; it was my faulty expectations.

I was looking for a perfect Savior. And none of them could be that person.

Something in my early Christian formation taught me to elevate my fellow human beings beyond their God-given capacities. I placed on them my superhuman expectations. What I needed to learn and relearn again and again is that only God is all-powerful (omnipotent), all-present (omnipresent), and all-knowing (omniscient). We are not. In the next chapter, we will look at these three ways in which humans are *unlike* God. This is a necessary first step before we consider practices and strategies that can help us learn *how* to embrace our limits and the good news they bring to our lives.

CHAPTER 3

HUMANS ARE UNLIKE GOD

Many years ago there was a man named John. John struggled with deep doubts about his faith in God. But he did not let the tension between his faith and his doubts paralyze him. John's ambition led him to accomplish extraordinary tasks. Extraordinary.

John traveled widely to spread the gospel. He traveled via the best method available during his time: on a horse. He rode a lot. More specifically, he rode 250,000 miles on his horse to spread the gospel. That's the equivalent of circling the earth ten times, all in his efforts to evangelize. As he rode, John read books to educate and enrich himself to further his mission. During his preaching career, which lasted more than sixty years, he preached over forty thousand sermons. Yes, John preached more than one sermon per day for over six decades. Every day. In fact, he preached closer to two sermons per day.

John believed that spreading the gospel also included helping people physically. He started health clinics for the poor and in 1747 wrote a medical text called *Primitive Physick: Or, An Easy and Natural Method of Curing Most Diseases.* He wrote this book in common, ordinary language so it could help as many people as possible. It went through thirty-eight editions and became one of the most widely read books in England, making it one of the all-time bestselling medical texts.

John was also a successful organizer. His Bible study group started in a small room at his university and grew into a movement that, at the time of his death, included seventy-two thousand members in the UK and sixty thousand in America.

By now you may have recognized the person I'm describing: John Wesley, born in England in 1703, the founder of Methodism. By all accounts, he accomplished a lot during his lifetime. You could say that he pushed the limits of what is humanly possible. His accomplishments make modern-day hustle gurus look like rookies.

I don't know about you, but when I hear about the achievements of people like John Wesley, I am impressed. I also get sad. I feel that way because I start playing the comparison game. I have started many Bible studies. Most of them have stopped, or fallen apart. None of them grew into multinational movements of thousands of people. But I'm not John, and neither are you. That was *his* story, *his* time, and *his* calling. It unfolded by God's power against the backdrop of human limits we all face. We aren't meant to play the comparison game; we *are* meant to go on our own adventures.

One of my hopes for this book is to inspire you to explore and engage how God has made *you*. God has you here for a reason. Yes, you have limitations. But knowing those limits will help you live a more healthy and balanced life, which is good news for accomplishing what God has for you.

AIM HIGH?

When I became a Christian in high school, my approach to school did not change immediately. The previous year, I was late to school over half the time. The front desk ladies had a soft spot for me and would kindly call me to wake me up and encourage me to come to school. Whenever I did make it to school, I did well on tests but rarely completed my homework. I passed my classes—barely. One of my new Christian friends challenged me to approach my schooling and schoolwork differently. She told me to do it for Christ, not for the teachers. I know that might sound cliché to some people, but it helped me! It gave me a new reason to do my best. My efforts to learn now had a greater purpose . . . and the front desk ladies were happier too.

Paul did not hide his effort and ambition to share the gospel. He wrote, "It has always been my ambition to preach the gospel where Christ was not known" (Rom. 15:20). God is not opposed to our effort and ambition. God *is* opposed to effort and ambition that are self-centered. Luke records Jesus as saying, "All those who exalt themselves will be humbled, and those who humble themselves will be exalted" (Luke 14:11). Pretty clear, right? When we seek to exalt ourselves, we will be humbled. Peter similarly wrote,

> All of you, clothe yourselves with humility toward one another, because,

"God opposes the proud
but shows favor to the humble."

Humble yourselves, therefore, under God's mighty hand,
that he may lift you up in due time. (1 Peter 5:5–6)

I don't know about you, but I am terrified of God opposing me; I know how that ends. I lose. Peter gave us a clear formula: if you want God to oppose you, be proud. Fortunately, he also told us how to experience God's favor: be humble.

I implore you, be humble by knowing your limits.

When I was in college, I lived in a house with my best friends. At some point we acquired boxing gloves and goofed around with them, all in good fun. One of my best friends, Daniel, asked if I wanted to have a friendly boxing match with him. I should have known my limits.

There are a few things you should know about Daniel. Daniel is one of the nicest, most thoughtful, and (most of the time) gentlest people I know. He loves Jesus and others. You should also know that Daniel was an all-state athlete in high school and played college football. Oh, and Daniel bench-pressed over four hundred pounds. I, on the other hand, taught myself how to program my computer as a kid. Let's just say I wasn't bench-pressing four hundred pounds.

Seconds after Daniel and I tapped gloves, he hit me square in the chest. I fell backward. He had knocked the wind right out of me. I was done—in one punch! Daniel was shocked and came to my aid right away. One second. One punch. And one limit of which I should have been more aware: don't try to box Daniel.

You have different skills and strengths than I do. We are all different. But there are some absolute human limits that all of us experience. I'm not talking about whether you are good at boxing. In the first chapter, I mentioned some limits that are specific to us, but there are also those that are more universal. No one is going to run a one-second mile. No one can be physically present at a rugby match, a dance competition, and a cross-country meet held at different locations all at the same time. And no one can know every bit of trivia on *Jeopardy!*

Knowing the good news of our limits begins with knowing our limits. And three crucial limits apply to every person reading this book, regardless of your background, experiences, skills, gifts, or whatever makes you unique. I don't need to meet you to tell you that you aren't omnipotent, omnipresent, or omniscient. Let's take a closer look at what each of these means and why something so obvious still needs to be said.

NOT FUNNY (WE ARE NOT OMNIPOTENT)

Andy Kaufman was a comedian and actor from the early years of the TV show *Saturday Night Live*. He was an odd guy. Out of humor, or something else, he often played oddball, rude, and subtly-genius-while-terrible characters. Jim Carrey starred as Kaufman in *Man on the Moon*, a movie made about Kaufman's life. The final part of the movie follows Kaufman's search for a cure for his rare form of lung cancer. After all traditional medical options failed, Kaufman journeyed to a mystical psychic medical healer in a remote part of the Philippines. Amid an elaborate "surgery," Kaufman realizes that the surgery and the mystic psychic medical healer were all a hoax. The movie ends with

Kaufman laughing because the joke was on him. But I didn't laugh.

As I watched the movie, I wanted Kaufman to be healed. When Kaufman was unable to be healed, he laughed, but I cried. I didn't see Kaufman. I saw Troy. Troy was a close friend of mine who also died of cancer despite the best medical treatment and abundant prayers.

Garth Brooks sang that "some of God's greatest gifts are unanswered prayers."[1] Part of me agrees with good ol' Garth, but most of me, if I'm being honest, is mad at that song. I resonate more with Sufjan Stevens, who, in his song "Casimir Pulaski Day," describes his experience with a friend who died of cancer. Stevens sings about praying for his friend at a Tuesday night Bible study and ends his verse by lamenting, "But nothing ever happens." When it comes to expressing real pain, I prefer the unresolved honesty, tension, and frustration of Stevens over the optimism and happy resolution of Brooks. Maybe that's just me.

Our emergencies, challenges, difficulties, and heartbreaks slam us headfirst into the reality that we are not all-powerful. We are not in control. And we can't change everything we want to change. Theologians have a word for this craving for power we want but can't have: *omnipotence*. And you and I are *not* omnipotent. In reality, we are semi-potent. We have power over some circumstances, but not everything.

Jesus, being fully divine and fully God, is omnipotent. Jesus affirmed this when he told the rich young ruler, "With God all things are possible" (Matt. 19:26). We see Jesus's divine power on display in his miracles throughout the New Testament. But as we read the Gospels, we also see that Jesus did not heal and save everyone. Some people passed by Jesus, and some Jesus did not seek out (like the gentiles). Jesus let some people walk away. He did not go after them to bring them back, for whatever reason. Jesus did not leave every group of "ninety-nine" to go after the "one." There were many of the "ones" to whom Jesus did not go. Jesus did not resolve everything with a happy conclusion. He did not stop to minister to every person.

Mark wrote that Jesus "could not do any miracles [in Nazareth]" (Mark 6:5). Mark continued by saying that Jesus marveled at the unbelief of the people in that situation. We certainly should not jump to the conclusion that healing is always a result of human faith. Why not? Faith does not initiate healing because, plain and simple, we aren't God. And we cannot control God, even by the actualization of faith.

Okay, fine, we do not control God. But that does not explain fully what is happening in Mark 6, where Jesus could not do mighty works. I thought Jesus, as God, being omnipotent, could do anything. True. At the same time, a mysterious tension hangs in this passage. We will return to that in a moment.

As we read further in Mark, we see that Jesus did not succumb to the demands of the Pharisees who "asked him for a sign from heaven" (Mark 8:11). Similarly, Jesus did not come down from the cross as the chief priests and scribes mockingly requested (Mark 15:30). These are things Jesus *did not do*, though he *could* have.

Jesus turned down many requests, not only public miracles. Many of these could have been powerful displays of God's power, of Jesus's own power and identity, yet he declined. In addition to forgoing some public miracles, Jesus told the story of the ten virgins, only five of whom respond to the "wedding banquet" invitation (Matt. 25:1–13). The lingering five arrive at the closed door and ask to be let inside. They cry out, "Lord, Lord, open the door for us." The bridegroom answers, "I don't know you." Why doesn't Jesus let them in? When I read this passage, I want to yell out, "Let them in!" Jesus responds, "No." Jesus was trying to make the point that we need to be ready for his return, but in the parable we also see that Jesus does not do what he *could* do. We see a similar situation in Jesus's parable of the weeds (Matt. 13:24–30, 36–43).

Jesus's humanity gives us a model for our own human limits. We know we are not God. We know we can't control God. We also know, however frustrating, that God's decision to do, or *not* to do, something is beyond human comprehension. But amid everything we can't do, we observe in Jesus his divinity and his humanity. The incarnate human Jesus took on human limits. As we have discussed, Jesus was hungry (Matt. 4:2), thirsty (John 19:28), and tired (John 4:6). Further, he did not—and sometimes even "could not"—always do what we might want Jesus to do.

Hungry, thirsty, tired, unable to change the outcome of everything we want—this is what it means to be human. Our lack of omnipotence can be frustrating. But before I explain how we can embrace our semi-potent humanity, we need to look at another limit we face: no matter how hard we try, we can't be everywhere at once.

REFRESHING OUR INSTAGRAM FEEDS (WE ARE NOT OMNIPRESENT)

I grew up in an apartment and always had food on the table, thanks to my mom's waiting tables at a restaurant nearly every night. She often worked "doubles" too, adding lunch shifts to pay the bills. But we didn't travel or vacation often—that wasn't a part of our reality. I attended a "rich" high school because of an interesting way the school boundaries were designed. The cars in the student parking lot at my high school were much nicer than those in the teachers' parking lot. When I arrived at my high school, it felt like I had pulled up to the school in *Beverly Hills, 90210*, one of my favorite TV shows growing up.

Most families at my high school had money, yet they rarely traveled outside the country. I can recall only one student I knew who went on a big trip. She went to Paris with her family over the summer. Things have changed since the early 1990s. Now people travel . . . a lot.

In our modern age, we enjoy more and more access to nearly anywhere we want to be. We can be present in different ways because of advances in travel (for example, affordable cars, cheap airfare, improved international travel), written communication (for example, postal service, text messages, email), audio communication (for example, telephones, long distance phone calls, international phone calls, cell phones), as well as video communication (Skype, FaceTime, Zoom, and so on). I believe these wonderful advances in technology have also brought a curse. I call this the curse of "everywhereness." We think we can be pretty much anywhere at any time. But we can't. This is beyond our limits.

God existed before any created "space" existed. Before we talk about space and location, it's important to know that God transcends all "locatedness." Before any location came to be, God existed and created the heavens and the earth (Gen. 1:1). Ever since the creation of the world, God exists throughout all creation, every square inch, all the time. God proclaimed rhetorically through Jeremiah, "Do not I fill heaven and earth?" (Jer. 23:24).

Is there a secret location, perhaps a cave or an island, or even some sort of otherworldly place where God isn't already there? No. The psalmist teaches us,

> If I go up to the heavens, you are there;
> If I make my bed in the depths, you are there.
> (Ps. 139:8)

God does not need a passport. God does not travel. God is already anywhere you can think of right now, and everywhere you can't think of, and has been there forever. Deists—those who believe God created the world like a machine, started it, and then stepped away—confine God to a distant heaven. Wrong. Polytheists—those who believe in multiple gods—confine God to certain places here and there. Wrong. Pantheists—those who see God in everything—confine God to creation itself. Wrong. God is *not* his creation. He transcends it. Yet he is omnipresent in all his creation and beyond.

You might concede my point and say, "Okay, I get it; God is omnipresent and humans are not." Yes, it's true. But many of us have not let this truth sink into our hearts. We feel the pull of being everywhere, of doing it all, and want to avoid the fear of missing out (FOMO). We have been convinced by our friends' curated social media travel highlights, the connectivity of our smartphones, and perhaps our own travels that we can, and maybe should, be able to be anywhere, perhaps everywhere, we want to be. We long for the impossible, for serene island vacations or almost anything different from our daily reality. The grass is always greener on the other side of our social media feed. But more significantly, we expect more of ourselves than is humanly possible. We want to be physically present in more than one place at a time. We want to be God.

The temptation of the garden echoes yet again in each of our lives.

When we are at work, we want to be elsewhere, and so we use technology to approximate omnipotence. We pull up pictures of a different location on our phone. When we are speaking with someone right in front of us, we may wish we were with someone else, and that becomes possible by sending a quick text message or taking a peek at our phone. When we are at home, we feel like being somewhere else, and that can be done by ordering an Uber to shuttle us across town. Are any of these inherently bad? No. But they are idolatrous pathways by which the lure of omnipotence—being like God—captures our heart. We fail to focus on where we are and who we are with. We disregard, overlook, and disrespect where God has already placed us right *here* and right *now*.

The majority of Jesus's life was spent in a relatively small geographic area. A two-hour drive, as the crow flies, could take us from Bethany, the southernmost city of Jesus's ministry, to Tyre and Sidon, the northernmost area of his ministry. From east to west, the area of Jesus's travels was narrow, perhaps as little as thirty miles wide. The earth has over fifty-seven million square miles of land, which is about 29 percent of its total surface. Jesus's entire ministry inhabited fewer than four thousand square miles, or roughly 0.007 percent of the land on earth. God's strategic plan for the redemption of the entire cosmos occurred on one small speck of the earth.

Jesus was certainly aware of other locations to which he *could* have gone. I'm sure Mary and Joseph told him of his time in Egypt as an infant. Jesus, like everyone in the Roman Empire, would have heard many details of other cities in the empire, not the least of which was Rome. And as a Jew, he would have heard a lot about the history of Jewish people in Egypt and of the Babylonian exile.

Jesus didn't use a cheat code to transport himself to his destinations; he endured the sweat and callouses of walking long distances from one place to the next. The gospel accounts are full of the details of his journeys, and Jesus made the most of this time. He taught. He listened. He encountered people he wouldn't have met if he teleported himself place to place. He stopped. He continued. Jesus embraced the entire experience of slow, limited, and interrupted travel.

Jesus's limited presence during his ministry made life difficult for others as well.

For example, in John 11, Jesus knows that his friend Lazarus is dying, yet he takes several days to arrive and be physically present. In that time, Lazarus has died, waiting for Jesus to get there. Jesus goes on to raise Lazarus from the dead and uses this situation to foreshadow his own resurrection. Yet the particulars of this story were all a by-product of the fact that Jesus's life on earth was limited. He could be in only one place at a time, even when the life of a dear friend was at stake.

In Luke 8 Jesus is on his way to heal a twelve-year-old girl who is dying. Jesus pauses and delays his journey to listen to an outcast—a perpetually sick, bleeding woman—whom he heals. When Jesus continues his journey and arrives at the house of the little girl, he is too late. She had died (Luke 8:53). Yet Jesus raises her from the dead. In this case, Jesus's physical presence was integral to the healing.

The Gospels also show us that Jesus healed from a distance. Jesus healed the daughter of a woman even though her daughter wasn't physically present with Jesus (Mark 7:24–30; Matt. 15:21–28). He healed the servant of a centurion in a similar way (Matt. 8:5–13; Luke 7:1–10). This also happened to an official's son in John 4:46–54. While Jesus wasn't physically present with those he healed in these situations, we should note that the mother, centurion, and official were with Jesus. All these people lived within 0.007 percent of the land on earth that Jesus roamed during his ministry. They benefited from the limited human presence of Jesus Christ. Certainly, there were other people on earth in those exact same moments who would have longed for Jesus Christ in the midst of their emergencies, yet Jesus wasn't physically present with them.

The power of God is *never* limited to one small speck of the universe. God is both omnipotent and omnipresent. God's presence is not limited; human presence *is* limited. This is what we learn from the life of Jesus as we focus our theological bifocals on the two natures of Christ: human *and* divine. In the Gospels, we see Jesus *embracing* the limits of being human. He walks in a limited area. He is late because his trip took an unexpected twist. He is accessible *only* to those who are around him. He didn't bend the rules of being human; he embodied them. He modeled how to live a limited human life. The human life of Jesus Christ is our guide for living with our own limited capacities.

MORE DATA THAN WILL EVER BE VIEWED (WE ARE NOT OMNISCIENT)

We all struggle to be present, maybe because of the overwhelming waves of information overload. It is almost as if anything we could want to know is available in the palms of our hands. But is it really?

Scientists expect that in 2025, every connected person in the world will have 4,900 digital data engagements every day. That's about one digital interaction every eighteen seconds. Who predicted this? The people whose jobs depend on it. These scientists design hard drives and all sorts of ways to store information. They have to look forward because they have to invent, create, and build the products their customers desire. Whether they know it or not, customers— *human* customers—desire data, a lot of data.

In 1944 librarian Fremont Rider estimated that libraries were doubling their capacity every sixteen years. He estimated that by the year 2040, the Yale Library would require six thousand miles of shelves and a library staff of over six thousand people. One librarian per mile? Ambitious.

Rider's worries about shelf space didn't materialize, thanks to advances in technology. Scientists discovered ways to put data on materials other than the paper pages of books. In 1965 Gordon Moore predicted that the density of transistors would double about every two years. This meant that information storage density (how much information could be stored, for example, in every square inch) would double in capacity about every two years. The figure turned out to be every eighteen months! This came to be known as Moore's Law. Moore has accumulated a net worth of over $12 billion because he was right. Well, he was right for a few decades. In 2005 Moore said he was "flabbergasted" because in less than a decade, hard disks had increased their capacity a thousandfold. The trajectory for this new projection was labeled Kryder's Law, after scientist Mark Kryder.

Scientists started asking practical and, perhaps unknowingly, profound theological questions about data and information. A leading scientist delivered a paper in 1980 at the Institute of Electrical and Electronics Engineers symposium on "mass storage systems," entitled "Where Do We Go from Here?"[2] He argued that data expands to fill the space available. He believed that more and more data was being stored in the world because users couldn't identify obsolete and unneeded data. A few years later, another scientist concluded that the typical piece of information will *never be looked at by a human being.* Let that sink in. We have created technology that stores more pieces of information than is humanly possible to consume. Think of all the photos you have on your past and current phones; do you know which images are no longer needed?

The Bible teaches us that God "knows everything" (1 John 3:20). He knows everything about you. God "knows the secrets of the heart" (Ps. 44:21). God knows "when I sit and when I rise; you perceive my thoughts from afar" (Ps. 139:2). God "knows your hearts" (Luke 16:15). God "knows what you need before you ask him" (Matt. 6:8). God knows the future: "New things I declare; before they spring into being I announce them to you" (Isa. 42:9). God foretells "the former things long ago, my mouth announced them and I made them known; then suddenly I acted, and they came to pass" (Isa. 48:3). All those bits of information that data scientists say no one will ever encounter—yes, God knows those too.

The all-knowing God threw us a curveball when the Son of God became one of us in the person Jesus of Nazareth. Human beings are not all-knowing. So what happens when the all-knowing Son of God takes on not-all-knowing humanity? We don't have to guess at the answer. The Gospels tell us what happened. Jesus said, "About that day or hour [the "end of the age"] no one knows, not even the angels in heaven, nor the Son, but only the Father" (Matt. 24:36; Mark 13:32). Wait . . . the Son does not *know* when heaven and earth will pass away, but the Father does? How is this possible? If the Son and the Father, along with the Spirit, are "one" within the Trinity, shouldn't they know the same information?

Theologians have taken some swings at this curveball. One answer is that Jesus's assertion about his own lack of knowledge is simply an incomprehensible mystery. It could be that, because of the cosmos-rending significance of this divine data point, two of the three persons of the Trinity willingly consent to ignorance in this one, exceptional matter. Another answer is that Jesus willingly took on a self-limitation during his earthly ministry. Jesus is always equal with God in every way, but when Jesus emptied himself for his incarnational mission and "took on" humanity, he did so voluntarily (Phil. 2:5–11; see also Heb. 2:9; Col. 2:9).

My work with junior high students might help us understand how to think about this self-limitation. One of the benefits of working with these students is that I tend to be better than most of them at sports. I'm six-foot-four and coached elite-level high school basketball for a decade. I'm not a great athlete, but when I play against five-foot-five twelve-year-olds, I can win against most of them. My guilty pleasure is to play basketball with them on low-rimmed "dunk hoops." If we play one-on-one basketball, I can easily dominate almost any junior high student. But I try not to overdo it. Since my purpose for being with these students is for *both* of us to have fun and enjoy our time together, I don't do everything I *could* do on the basketball court—I self-limit.

Self-limiting is a tactic used to achieve a greater purpose. And when you are the eternal Son of God, what is that purpose? Theologians who advocate the self-limiting approach see Jesus's self-limitation as a means of fully embracing his humanity. In becoming human, the Son of God modeled reliance on the Father and the Spirit to show us, through the human limitations of being Jesus of Nazareth, that this is how we were meant to live. We are encouraged to take the same approach.

Another view is that since Jesus was fully human, he needed to experience real, human (limited) capacities too. So when we see Jesus not knowing something, we see evidence of his genuine humanity. At other times, when we see Jesus knowing what humans don't normally know, such as details about future events (Mark 11:2; John 1:48–49) or what other people are thinking (Mark 2:8), we see Jesus's divinity showing through. In this interpretation, we see glimpses of Jesus's humanity and divinity at different times in the Gospels.

At the end of the day, theologians don't agree exactly on how this all works out. And we aren't going to solve this mystery anytime soon. Here is our takeaway: If Jesus did not claim to know everything he "could" know, should we? Not only is there information we cannot know, more importantly, with our limited capacity for knowledge, we must also be wise in what we choose and seek to know. Jesus did not try to know everything possible in his world in his day. And that is a strong indication that we shouldn't either.

When I was a postgraduate student, I asked to meet with one of my professors, Tom "N. T." Wright. He kindly agreed and bought me some tea at Zest Café before we walked across the street to his office. After I finished asking some detailed questions about my future PhD research, I asked him if he had any general advice about being a scholar of Christianity. His advice was fascinating.

Tom told me there was once a time when he could keep up-to-date on all the various aspects of his specialized field of Pauline studies. But Tom confessed to me that he can't keep up anymore. Too much information is produced every day—even in the specialized field of Pauline studies—for him to know it all. He advised me to be selective in what I studied and to learn to be content with having partial information, even within my specialized field. At first I was shocked. Tom Wright was admitting that he had stopped trying to know everything he could know about the apostle Paul. The reason was simple, honest, and humble. No one *can* know everything being said about Paul these days. At first I wanted to throw in the towel on my own field of research. If Tom can't know it all, how could I ever hope to? But after deeper reflection, I felt relieved. Tom had given me permission to be human.

RECALIBRATE WITH ME

So what will happen if you try to be omnipotent, omnipresent, or omniscient? Easy. You will fail. And it will likely take a massive toll on your life.

You will fail because you don't have the equipment to succeed. Your failure is guaranteed, so I beg you to recalibrate your understanding of yourself and your capabilities back to reality—your God-given reality. Anyone can do this. Everyone *has* to do this. Time runs out. Tasks pile up. Opportunities are missed.

Our *human nature* is constrained by our abilities and our lack of abilities. So don't be offended. This isn't a *you* thing; this is a *human* thing. Failure greets us every day, and what do we say back to it? We must assess what is humanly possible and know what is beyond our limits.

But here is where our limits begin to be good news for us because the act of reassessing our capacities is an act of worship. We lay down our pride, our self-confidence, and our trust in our own strength and take an honest look at ourselves. We humbly realign our self-expectations and take up a new vision of our purpose and abilities. We silence internal whispers of failure and amplify messages of truth and health. We lay down our idolatry of self, which has already failed us many times over, and we lift up our dependence and obedience to the all-powerful, all-present, all-knowing Father, Son, and Holy Spirit. I need this recalibration as much as anyone. Learning how to recalibrate is the focus of the next few chapters of this book as we learn three practical ways to embrace our limits.

CHAPTER 4

THE FIRST LIMIT: FAITHFUL PRACTICES

Earlier today, I spoke with a friend and mentioned that my dog, whom we named after a friend in the United Kingdom, is difficult to take on walks because he gets incredibly distracted. Then, an hour later, I opened up one of my social media apps and saw an advertisement for "Awesome Dogs: the complete guide to training your unruly dog to do better on walks."

Now, isn't that strange? Have you ever had something like that happen?

And the kicker? The price was in British pounds: "Normally priced: £34.94. Today only: £13.80."

I don't know how these advertisements, or "adverts" as my UK friends say, show up on my phone. My suspicion is that I agreed to something in fine print somewhere that allows them to listen to me—and that freaks me out—but that is another story. Ten to fifteen years ago, this would never have happened.

Companies and advertisers didn't have the data, information, or tools available today. They had to make educated guesses to figure out the next thing that we *might* say yes to. Today they just listen in as we unwittingly tell them what we want.

You have probably noticed that you are hounded by advertisements. But you are also hounded by a not-so-subtle psychology that is prevalent today. It seeks to persuade us, to make us think we should say yes to almost everything. And if we say yes, the world will open up before us in amazing ways. All our wildest dreams will come true. But *is* this true?

JUST SAY YES? NOT QUITE

Hollywood captured the roller-coaster ride of saying yes to everything in the 2008 romantic comedy *Yes Man*. Carl Allen (played by Jim Carrey) is a relentlessly negative man with a job that suits him quite well: he is a loan officer determined to decline all loans. Carl is urged to attend a self-help seminar led by a persistent guru who convinces the attendees to say yes to everything—absolutely everything. Carl commits to saying yes at all costs, and hilarity ensues. The moral of the story isn't difficult to imagine: saying yes to everything creates problems (especially, in this case, with Carl's girlfriend Allison, played by Zooey Deschanel). The movie ends with Carl pledging to live a more honest and balanced life.

Some people are able to master several skills or areas of study at a high level. They can say yes to many commitments, and this somehow works for them. For example, Leonardo da Vinci has been described as a Renaissance man or polymath, someone who has a high level of knowledge or skill in several disciplines.

A modern example of a polymath includes Story Musgrave. Musgrave holds degrees in mathematics, computer science, chemistry, medicine, physiology, literature, and psychology, as well as twenty-one honorary doctorates. He was a mechanical engineer, US Special Forces aviator, clinical surgeon, and a practicing physiologist. He was the first person to complete a space walk from the space shuttle and the only person to fly aboard all five space shuttles as a NASA astronaut. Yet even with Musgrave's amazing competencies, he couldn't do *everything*. For example, he never received a call to play in the NBA. We share that in common.

While there is some pressure to master many interests and activities, like Musgrave, on the other end of the spectrum is an unfortunate push to hyperfocus on just a few topics, becoming overly specialized. I see this all the time today in high school athletics.

For more than ten years, I coached basketball at one of the largest and most successful high schools in Arizona. Most of our best players were multisport athletes, which went contrary to the advice many of them received. They were told that if they wanted to succeed, they should focus on one sport—to the exclusion of others. Now, I will grant that some sports lend themselves to specialization, such as gymnastics. But many athletes benefit from playing multiple sports. If you consider the statistics for Division I college athletes, 71 percent of football players, 88 percent of male lacrosse players, 83 percent of female lacrosse players, 87 percent of female runners, and 91 percent of male runners were multisport athletes.[1] Being a multisport athlete meant they stopped one sport to focus on another, and as it turns out, depending on your goals, it might be best *not* to isolate your focus to only one sport. Focusing too much on one thing, in this case, might be detrimental to success.

The *New York Times* bestselling books lists on productivity, goal setting, and human efficiency have a common thread that runs through them: *focus*. Stephen Covey's *7 Habits of Highly Effective People* instructs us to schedule and focus our time on our top priorities (putting the big rocks in the jar before filling it with sand). Timothy Ferriss's *The 4-Hour Workweek* provides vision and tips for committing to the required outcomes of our day jobs in order to free our time for other activities. David Allen provides specific steps and systems to maximize personal efficiency in his book *Getting Things Done*. Readers eagerly pick up the latest book in search for a panacea for our busyness, exhaustion, and frequent disappointment in our outcomes—readers like *me*.

I find these books incredibly helpful. I'm always eager to "sharpen the saw" (one of Covey's seven habits). But I believe these books, as helpful as they are, are missing something. They fail to account for theological anthropology—or to put it simply, they don't consider what it means for human beings to be created by a Creator.

Christians believe there is intentionality and design in the way God made humanity. The books I described are helpful. They will assist you in fixing and modifying your life so you can work faster and more efficiently. There is nothing wrong with that. I want to drive a dependable and efficient car. And occasionally, I admit, I like to floor my 2014 Honda Accord to see what it can do on the freeway. But there are limits to the performance and longevity of my Accord. If I wanted to know how to get the most out of my Accord, it would make sense to talk to the experts at Honda who designed my car. They would likely admit that my Accord was never designed to go one thousand miles per hour, and it won't last me over one hundred years of constant use. It wasn't designed that way.

God has designed you and me to live within our limits. We do this by restricting ourselves to a selective and focused *number* and *quality* of faithful practices.

JUST SAY NO? NOT QUITE

Malcolm Gladwell released his bestselling book *Outliers* in 2008. When I last checked, well over a decade after its release, this book was still a top seller in the category of "Decision-Making & Problem-Solving." The book includes a thirty-four-page chapter entitled "The 10,000-Hour Rule." As Gladwell explains it, this rule suggests that ten thousand hours of focused practice will result in achieving world-class expertise in any skill. Gladwell's argument thrived when *Outliers* first released because people found the guideline easy to understand, exciting, and visionary. If you have something you want to excel at, simply log the hours in a focused way, and—poof!—you're an expert!

But scientists and other critics were quick to push back against Gladwell's claim. They argued that Gladwell generalized his concept far too much and did not take into account many factors, including genetic makeup, the age at which you start learning something, and how you learn. As it turns out, even Gladwell concedes that you can put in the hours and still be . . . mediocre. I have certainly put in over ten thousand hours practicing and playing basketball. But the NBA hasn't called me yet. Though I can beat *most* junior high kids.

My takeaway from Gladwell's thesis is not that you are guaranteed to become an expert, but that focus—specific, intentional focus—creates results. Gladwell and his naysayers all agree that learning takes time. Things that matter, things that are important, and things that bring joy to us and others require prolonged dedication, time, and focus. Further—and this is critically important as we think about our limits—this investment comes at the expense of other alternatives in which you did *not* invest your focus, time, and dedication. There is *always* a trade-off. When you are practicing the violin, you aren't going skydiving. Everyone has the same twenty-four hours. We can't create more time.

So is the key to embracing our God-given limits as simple as saying no to some opportunities and yes to others? Not entirely.

Computer scientist and author Cal Newport learned how to embrace his limits. He is the author of some of the best books on productivity in the modern world. One of those books is titled *Deep Work*, and Newport argues that deep and focused work is one of the most sought after and rare abilities in the modern age because of the abundance of shallow distractions and busywork. He claims that those who master two core abilities will thrive in the new economy. First, they must develop the ability to quickly master hard tasks, and second, they must learn how to produce at an elite level, in terms of quality and speed. The first discipline Newport instructs his readers to adopt is to "focus on the wildly important."[2] He believes that the more we try to do, the less we accomplish. Newport's research concludes that deep work occurs when we identify a small number of ambitious outcomes to pursue.

I'll lay my cards on the table and say I think Newport is right. The wisest way to embrace our inherent human limitations is to choose a small number of "wildly important" tasks and habits that will accomplish our desired outcomes. But this leads us to a serious and important question, one you will need to answer for yourself in collaboration with the Holy Spirit: *What is the desired outcome of my life?* After you have answered that, or at least taken a stab at it, then you should select a small number of tasks and habits that will lead you to this outcome.

We know God did not design us to say yes to everything; that is beyond our design. We also know God did not design us to say no to everything; that is beneath our design. To embrace our limits, we must learn how to say yes to a limited number of faithful practices that lead us to what God wants for our lives.

WHEN YOU DON'T KNOW WHAT TO SAY

I became a Christian during my junior year of high school. Prior to that moment, I had no place for God in my life—or in my calendar either. The following year, my senior year of high school, was very different.

On Mondays I had a Bible study group at lunch. Somehow I was now the president of that group and was in charge of arranging the speakers. I also designed, ordered, collected the money for, and distributed the T-shirts we wore. Most importantly, I ordered and collected the money for the pizza each week. And each Monday night, I went to Young Life. I showed up early and stayed late.

On Tuesdays I got ready for the rest of the week.

On Wednesdays I went to my church's youth group. I was also part of the student leadership team there. This meant I came early for a meal and a leadership meeting, and then I stayed late. I also played the drums in the youth group worship band.

On Thursdays I woke up early to go to Fellowship of Christian Athletes. I wasn't much of an athlete, but they let me in anyway. I never missed a meeting. The Bible studies and fellowship were good, and so were the donuts. On Thursday nights I went to "big church" worship practice. The church had realized that my drumming in youth group was just good enough not to mess up "big church" worship. Worship practice consisted of two hours of team members telling the drummer (me) to keep quiet while they tuned their guitars, wrote down chord changes, and figured out harmonies among the singers. I eventually just brought a book and hit the crash cymbal every so often to let them know I was still there. Sometime during my senior year, I realized I had no real grasp of my newfound Christianity, so I joined a theology class at my church before worship practice on Thursday nights.

On Fridays I helped lead Young Life for junior high students at my old middle school. This was the highlight of the week. It was so much fun. At least the school week was over.

On Saturdays my energetic friends often talked me into going to ubercharismatic quasi churches that met at motels near the airport off and on. I didn't know what to make of it, and still don't, but it was nice because it was one of the few events I simply attended.

On Sundays I woke up much earlier than normal to arrive at church for worship band practice. After practice and two church services, my friends and I would go to a long lunch. Once a month our church held a Sunday night prayer and worship service. Guess who was the drummer?

I look back at my senior year of high school with fond memories. It was a foundational and dynamic time for my spiritual growth. Many of the people I met and the lessons I learned that year shaped the rest of my life. No one made me take on these responsibilities. I simply kept saying yes.

In comparison to my junior year, however, I had added an incredible number of commitments. All these activities were new to me and my weekly schedule. Looking back, I have no idea how I did it all. During my senior year, I maintained my existing junior year commitments, including a part-time job, playing two varsity sports, dating a nice Christian girl (now my wife), and, oh, being a student and a son to my single mother. After high school, I went to college nearby and kept nearly all those same commitments, or I replaced them with college ministry versions. I established a routine and habits that worked for me. Until they didn't.

In my short Christian experience up to that point, I and those around me praised, encouraged, and celebrated my commitments and routines. I had not reached a breaking point. I didn't have any single experience that forced me to reassess my commitments. I just knew something wasn't right. All these undertakings felt right, individually. They were all good things. But I knew I had to stop. I had to eliminate. I had to limit. And that's when something unexpected happened.

I asked my youth pastor if I could meet him before our Wednesday night youth group leadership meeting. When I walked in, I sat down and started to talk. And then, unexpectedly, I started crying. I don't cry much. But on that Wednesday, I did—a lot. Something was wrapped up inside me, but I couldn't explain it. I didn't have it figured out. I knew that the combination of all these commitments I had made wasn't good for me. It was as if my body and spirit had said "stop." When I didn't know what to say, because I didn't understand it, my body and spirit told me what I needed.

I felt terrible. I felt like I had let down my wonderful, wise, and compassionate youth pastor, one of my heroes who had believed in me from day one. But I also felt relieved. A sense of health and well-being reentered my body and soul as tears ran down my face. On that day, embracing my limits was painful. For me, it always is.

KEN VENTURI'S GOLF TIPS

Golf is a difficult sport. The average golf swing takes about one second. Moving the golf club back, the backswing, takes about three quarters of a second. Moving the club down to hit the ball, the downswing, takes about a quarter of a second.

I grew up in a neighborhood of apartments and condominiums in Scottsdale, Arizona, that was a sought-after destination for "snowbirds." The snowbirds are mostly older, retired folks who make the annual trek from frigid places like Canada and Minnesota to sunny Arizona for the winter. The license plates announce their arrival each winter. My neighborhood had two seasons. Season one was mostly empty apartments and condos. Season two was snowbird season. As an only child with a mom who was waitressing double shifts most days, I was alone a lot, and I was bored—a lot. I discovered ways to keep busy, like teaching myself to program a computer.

One day I found my grandma's old Laura Baugh golf clubs and some hollow, plastic practice golf balls that went about ten feet when you hit them. On the weekends, I began watching golf on TV. I would pause everything I was doing when my favorite segment came on. Prior to the commercials, they would show Ken Venturi's golf tips. After watching these, I would run and grab one of my grandma's golf clubs and imitate Ken's tips in front of my TV. Then I would rush out to the grassy area in my neighborhood and practice hitting my hollow, plastic golf balls using Ken's latest tip. Occasionally, a kind snowbird would chirp out, "Nice swing!" I was hooked.

Now, three decades later, I am still hooked. And I still hook a lot of my golf shots too. That is one of the beautiful and humiliating challenges of golf: it is impossible to golf perfectly. The lowest golf score ever recorded in a professional tournament is fifty-eight shots for eighteen holes. No one has come anywhere close to a "perfect" score of eighteen shots for eighteen holes.

One of the challenges of a golf swing is that it all happens so fast. The swing takes place faster than you can think or react. Golf is similar to many sports in that you develop habits, skills, and instantaneous reactions that occur in the blink of an eye. This book is not about golf, but I will give you one piece of advice as a freebie. The key to golf is the setup. If the setup for your golf swing is wrong, decades of good habits, skills, and instantaneous reactions can be wasted. The most important aspect of a good setup in golf is alignment toward the target—that is, aiming at the hole.

From time to time, golf courses will have two greens near each other. More than once, I have made an excellent golf swing, and the ball went right where I wanted. But as I walked closer to the hole, I discovered that I had hit the ball onto the wrong green.

There are many intricacies to a high-quality setup in a golf swing: your grip; how your feet are spaced; the bend in your knees, hips, and spine; your aim; and more. The setup for a good swing requires that many elements be considered and mastered.

If your golf swing needs improvement, work on your setup. Why? You have much longer than one second for your setup. You can take as long as you need to get it right. But once you swing, you have only one second.

To embrace the limits of your power, to reconcile what you *could* do with what you *should* do, work on your setup. Work on your aim. Life comes at us so fast that it is hard for us to react correctly if we're not prepared. Golf instructors recommend that you think about only one thing during your one-second swing; they call this a "swing thought." In the span of one second, your brain can probably process only one thought that might help your golf swing.

Why are we talking about golf? Because each one of us needs to consider what that one "swing thought" will be for our lives. Here's a place to start. Jesus commanded us to think one thought above all other thoughts, one split-second habit, skill, and instantaneous reaction to focus on in the midst of lives that move at breakneck speed: *love*. According to Jesus, love is the "swing thought" for the life of faith. Love the Lord your God, and love your neighbor as yourself. Make that your instantaneous reaction all day long.

The work of embracing your limits falls almost entirely on how you set up the norms of your life. And the good news is that for this task, you have plenty of time—much more than one second.

SETUP: GOD GOALS AND FAITHFULNESS GOALS

A simple adjustment to your goals and aims can help you recalibrate what you *could* do with what you *should* do. Christians, churches, ministries, and small groups make a fundamental mistake when they think about what they want to accomplish. Their goals and aims rarely take into account how God intentionally made humans limited. Some utilize the approach of making their goals SMART (specific, measurable, achievable, realistic, and timely), and I would agree that this approach can be helpful. But I recommend taking a theological approach that is calibrated to the differences between God's capacities and human capacities. This approach can shift the "realistic" aspect of SMART goals in a more biblical direction.

The simple adjustment I'm recommending builds off Paul's words to the Corinthians: "I planted the seed, Apollos watered it, but God has been making it grow" (1 Cor. 3:6). Some people in the Corinthian church had become overinfatuated with Apollos, perhaps because he was eloquent, educated, dynamic, helpful, and powerful in public debates (Acts 18:24–28). Paul's point in the beginning of 1 Corinthians 3 isn't to debate the strengths and weaknesses of Paul or Apollos. Paul's purpose was to show the Corinthians that they were making a fundamental, categorical, and theological error: they were misunderstanding the different capacities of human beings and God.

Paul utilized an agricultural metaphor to correct the Corinthians: growing plants. Planting and watering are tasks that farmers can control. Farmers can get up every day and put seeds in soil and water them. But farmers *cannot* make plants grow.

I always smile when I think of when Happy Gilmore, from the classic golf comedy movie, hunched down on the putting green, whispering to his golf ball, "Go home. Are you too good for your home?!" to no avail. A farmer could get down next to the freshly watered seed and whisper, "Grow!" over and over, but it wouldn't change a thing. As Paul points out, he and Apollos could plant and water, yes, but they did not have the capacity to make *anything* grow. *Only* God can bring growth.

Much of my life has been devoted to youth evangelism. I deeply want teenagers to become disciples of Jesus Christ, and that begins when they become Christians at some point. Ministers in my circles have said things like, "This year I want to see five students come to Christ." Statements like this are great, beautiful, and wonderful but *impossible* as a human goal. Most of my colleagues know they can't "make" someone become a Christian, so they use tactics that contribute toward this goal. They might say, "I want to bring twenty-five students to weekend camp." That sounds doable, right? Last time I checked, you can't force anyone to go to a weekend camp—trust me, I've tried. Desperate youth ministers have become a caricaturized version of Happy Gilmore whispering, "Go to camp . . . go to camp . . . go to camp," to their students. Guess what? It does not work. It's the wrong approach.

We cannot control God. God is the only one who can bring salvation. And we can't control other people, no matter how much, for example, we beg them to go to a camp. What we learn from Paul, and what we need to focus on, is what we *can* control: ourselves (as best we can). We need to separate "God goals" from "faithfulness goals." The simple difference between God goals and faithfulness goals comes from the different capacities of God and humans. *God goals* are things that only God can do. *Faithfulness goals* are things that we can do and God will use. God is omnipotent—all powerful. Humans are semi-potent—somewhat powerful (and essentially different from God).

I challenge you to identify how a farmer might interpret "farmer faithfulness goals" in the verses below:

[The Lord] makes grass grow for the cattle,
  and plants for people to cultivate—
  bringing forth food from the earth.
    (Ps. 104:14)

[The Lord] covers the sky with clouds;
  he supplies the earth with rain
  and makes grass grow on the hills. (Ps. 147:8)

Farmer goals might include cultivating and preparing soil to grow the plants. A farmer has this capacity as a human. God goals include making grass and plants grow, covering the sky with clouds, and making it rain. God has these capacities; a farmer does not.

Identify how an evangelist might interpret "evangelist faithfulness goals" in this passage: "[Jesus] also said, 'This is what the kingdom of God is like. A man scatters seed on the ground. Night and day, whether he sleeps or gets up, the seed sprouts and grows, though he does not know how'" (Mark 4:26–27). Evangelist faithfulness goals might include "scattering seed," a metaphor for sharing the gospel. Another task of the evangelist is to sleep and wake up. God goals include sprouting the gospel seed in people's hearts and growing the kingdom of God. God has these capacities; an evangelist does not.

As we look at Jesus's life on earth, we see that he did not attempt to "do it all." While being fully God, Jesus exemplified a life of selective human faithfulness. Jesus didn't go far geographically. He didn't attempt to reach the Gentiles. Jesus did not try to save everyone—he left towns that were only partially evangelized, picking up and moving on to the next town. He waited until the last three years of his life to begin his ministry. So let me ask you, are you trying to be more faithful than Christ?

PRAY BIG, LIVE FAITHFULLY

My family has a sign placed prominently in our kitchen. It is one of those artsy chalkboard frames with a simple white font in all capital letters on a black background. It states, "PRAY BIG." I purchased it and hung it in our kitchen for my family and all our visitors to see. And I need to see it often too. I believe that many of our prayers aren't big enough. For some of us, this is because we envision God's capacities as simply an upgraded version of our own human capacities. We ask God for a "good" day. How bland and boring is that? Instead of praying for a good day, might we instead pray, "Your kingdom come . . . today, yes, today Lord. Do not delay."

Turning to God in prayer is how we should express our God goals. Unfortunately, I tend to have this practice exactly backward. I turn to prayer *after* my capacities have failed me. My prayers are typically the backup plan. My prayers are often requests to make my own efforts just a bit better than what I can do on my own. My prayers often reveal how much I think I can make God in my own image, rather than the other way around.

Prayer is our request for and praise of the character and capacities of the transcendent omnipotence of the Father, Son, and Holy Spirit. Prayer is the act of trading the futile sparks of a flint stone for the ever-burning, overwhelming ferocity of the sun at the center of our universe. Lay your God goals before God in prayer. Pray big. Pray expansively. Pray over and over. Then stop and let them be.

I have a snarky friend who famously told a guy he was discipling that he wouldn't pray for his prayer request. The young man had asked my friend, "Please pray that I can get my homework done." My friend threw it back at him, saying, "I won't pray for that." His young disciple looked up, shocked, surprised, and frustrated. Why would he not pray for this poor kid's struggle to do his homework? And the answer is because *the kid just needed to do his homework.* He had the time, the location, and the resources available—and now he just needed to do it. What this young disciple needed was to be faithful because this task was within his human capacity. In later prayer requests, my friend taught his young disciple to ask for prayer for things *beyond* his capacities, such as asking God to give him wisdom and to lead him away from temptations that might divert him from completing tasks like doing his homework.

The farmer does not need to pray about waking up and planting seed. The farmer can do that. The evangelist does not need to pray about sharing the gospel. The evangelist can do that. The farmer can pray for health and strength to wake up each day and do the work of planting. God alone can grant those blessings. The evangelist can pray for courage and wisdom to share the gospel, which God alone can grant. Anyone can ask the person in front of them, "What do you think of Jesus Christ?" It's as easy as asking the person, "What time is it?" It is simply a choice of words. This is a choice we can make. This is a choice of faithfulness that is within our capacities, at least when God is the one sculpting our desires and capacities by his indwelling Spirit.

GRADUATION NIGHT: LEARNING TO ASK, "WAS I FAITHFUL?"

I opened this book with the story of my experience attending a recent high school graduation. In past years, I often felt that graduation night confirmed my youth ministry failures. It was a reminder that I had failed to achieve my goal of reaching every student with the gospel or that I had led very few students into a relationship with Christ. Some of the graduating seniors to whom I ministered over the previous four years had regressed and backslid in their faith. Graduations evidenced my train wreck of personal failure and guilt. After graduation, when I returned to my car, I kept telling myself, "I need to do better."

I was wrong.

I had convinced myself that achieving these outcomes was within my capacities. I thought I could lead a person to Jesus. I could help kids thrive in their faith. I could control whether a student backslid. But none of this is true.

I have no control over these outcomes. Zero. *I am not God.* Only God has the power to accomplish these goals. I had confused God goals with faithfulness goals.

My recent epiphany at graduation helped me to start asking whether I was faithful in what I had control over. As I scanned across the rows of graduates, I recalled attempts I had made to attend cross-country meets and basketball games. I remembered times of prayer when I lifted up the names of dozens of students I had met. I was reminded of invitations I texted to students for Bible studies: some were returned, many were not. In sum, I asked myself "faithfulness questions." Don't get me wrong, I saw room for improvement in my faithfulness goals too, but at least I was beginning to ask the *right* questions. I embraced the tasks God had given me influence over. Also, I saw some of the answers to prayer in a new light. The students who *did* begin a relationship with Christ or grew in their faith were true miracles of God. My mind and heart praised God for what only he could do.

I am learning to embrace the limits of my capacities on a more personal level in my family as well. My wife and I are parents of three teenagers. Erin and I have prayed for our children from before they were born. We have prayed that our kids would know Jesus. I struggle with this reality, but I know I have no actual control over the faith life of my children. I can't control whether my children follow Jesus. It breaks my heart. I would do anything, and have tried everything, to control this. Yet this "goal" is simply not within Erin's or my capacities.

So we need to embrace our limited abilities to change circumstances in our lives. But that's not all. We must also learn to embrace our limited relational capacities. Spending two hours a week with a youth minister for four years may not have as much influence on a student as a decade or two of living at home with the rest of their family. In the next chapter, we will look at how we can leverage our limited capacity for people and friends in positive and healthy ways that fit our God-given design.

CHAPTER 5

THE SECOND LIMIT: CIRCLES OF FRIENDS

Confession: I love ESPN. I watched a lot of it growing up. I moved out of my mom's apartment when I was eighteen years old (that was about twenty-five years ago). Since then I have subscribed to cable TV for only a few months. I am not claiming any moral high ground in saying that. I just know my weaknesses: that I would watch *Sports Center* nonstop if I had ESPN and that I've saved some serious money by not having cable for twenty-five years.

For over ten years, our TV has been connected solely to a computer. It acts as a massive computer screen on a wall in our living room. The primary purpose of the TV is to function as a screen saver. It cycles through pictures—a lot of pictures. I'll spare you the details, but through the power of the "cloud" via Dropbox, pictures that we take with our phones end up on our TV in our living room. Throughout the day we see a wide assortment of pictures of people and places from the last decade or so. This setup is fun for us, and it often brings back great memories. But with every picture that brings a happy memory, another picture brings a silent cringe of regret.

Many of the photos remind me of someone I haven't talked to in years.

I was sitting in our living room yesterday when a picture on our TV caught my attention. For five seconds, I enjoyed a photo of my youngest daughter, who is now thirteen, when she was little. In the photo, she wore a princess dress—the type you get for Halloween but that your daughter decides to wear three to four days a week year-round. She had a fairy wand in her hand and wore plastic princess shoes.

Before I knew it, those five seconds concluded, and the screen saver moved to the next picture. I saw a photo of our family standing in front of St. Rule's Tower in St. Andrews, Scotland, one of our favorite places in the world. I could look at that picture all day.

The next picture was another great memory. It was a picture of me and my high-school-age friend Austin after his cross-country meet. Austin's shirt was soaked with sweat. His face was beaming with joy as his first-place medal hung around his neck. In my hands, I was holding the big sign I had made. I had written on it, "GO Aust-WIN!" After a second or two of transporting myself back to that moment a decade ago, I spent the next few moments thinking about the last time I had talked to Austin. The truth was, I couldn't remember.

Forgetting people is a difficult subject to talk about. I place a high priority on friendships. I think most people would agree that they too want to place a high priority on friendships. But, for me, losing track of people cuts deep. I have devoted most of my life to sharing the gospel with teenagers. Genuine relationships are at the core of my efforts to share the gospel. So when I see a picture of a long-forgotten teenage friend, I feel that I did something wrong. The picture is proof that I wasn't able to sustain the genuine friendship I once had. My living room TV is a daily reminder of my limited capacity for friendship. And it saddens me.

I used to think I was an underachiever when it came to friendship. After all, I am an only child, I began my adult career as an engineer (we aren't known as social butterflies), and I recharge by being alone. I wasn't surprised that I wasn't a natural at maintaining a large number of genuine friendships long term. I figured it was a "me" thing. As it turns out, it isn't a "me" thing at all. Limited capacity for friendship is a *human* thing. God designed humans in a way that limits how many people we can know. I knew this limitation in theory, but Robin Dunbar gave me a clue to help me understand *why* I must select a few circles of friends.

DUNBAR'S NUMBER

Robin Dunbar is a social psychologist at Oxford University who established what is known as "Dunbar's number." Dunbar argued that the size of human brains limits the number of genuine friendships to 150 people. He concluded, "There is a cognitive limit to the number of individuals with whom any one person can maintain stable relationships. . . . [These] depend on extensive personal knowledge based on face-to-face interaction for their stability and coherence through time."[1] Personal knowledge and face-to-face interaction are required to belong within this group of friends. Dunbar showed that humans relate differently in groups of one to two, five, fifteen, fifty, one-hundred fifty, five hundred, fifteen hundred, five thousand, and beyond.

The first group is "Level 0." This group is one to two people. The easiest way to think of Level 0 is the person or two who might hold your hand when you die. This might be your parent or spouse.

My friend Curt and I were taking a break from making breakfast sandwiches while serving at a summer camp a few years ago. Brandon, Curt's brother, had recently died. He had been far too young. As Curt and I were enjoying a quiet moment eating our egg sandwiches, he asked me, "Have you heard the song 'What Sarah Said' by Death Cab for Cutie?" I had. It is a great song. I knew it as a song, but Curt knew it as an experience.

Singer and songwriter Benjamin Gibbard wrote lyrics to paint a somber picture of spending the last moments in the ICU with his friend Sarah. The song concludes: "love is watching someone die, so who's gonna watch you die?" My friend had been the answer to that question. Curt had been with Brandon as he was dying. When we think of our friendships, we often rush past the intimate inner circle of those dearest to us. But Dunbar helps us pinpoint the people who matter most. Think about it this way: If the moment of death came to you soon, who would be with you in those last moments?

The second group Dunbar identifies is called a "sympathy group" of five people. These are people who would do whatever it takes to visit you in the hospital and those few people you would turn to for advice, comfort, or help in a challenging, perhaps life-changing, situation. For many of us, these are our closest family members and perhaps a best friend or life mentor. Note that this group wouldn't be big enough for your entire extended family, and it already includes your Level 0 relationships.

Identifying our "sympathy group" is where the uncomfortable delineation, and gracious exclusion, of friendship groups begins. This step is easier to avoid than to work through, but if we want to take our limited capacity for relationships seriously, as I believe we should, making these distinctions in the innermost circles of friendship will help us give the time and attention to those who truly matter most. If we fail to identify these people, we risk trading them for a passerby.

The next group, made up of around fifteen people, is called a "squad." The term *squad* is taken from the typical size of a squad from the army. The squad naturally emerges through friendship, family, parenting, play, love, "group think" decision-making, and work. The emotional depth of this group can vary considerably. For instance, your squad could include casual friends on a sports team, a mentor or mentee, or an actual army squadron. These relationships have weathered an intense experience or season that cemented friendships with deep anchors.

Dunbar labels the next group "close friends," which includes fifty people. This is a group of people you might invite to your birthday party, graduation party, additional relatives, friendly acquaintances, some in-laws, some local club or work colleagues, and a few neighbors. You may have seen these people or sent them a text once or twice this week. Note that this group already includes the other groups of people in the previous group. So after your Level 0, sympathy group, and squad, this group tacks on only thirty-five more people. You are often together with these people without needing to put time with them "in your schedule."

The next group is the most significant for most of us because it is where determining the level of commitment to the relationship is most difficult. This group is the 150 people you would likely call your "friends." You recall their names quickly. You can pick up your friendship where you left off. If you saw this person with another group, you would feel comfortable going up, uninvited, and interrupting them to say hi. If you can easily or actively avoid this person when you see them, they aren't in this group. If you recognize their face, name, and some shared history together but feel like you could sneak right past them, they probably aren't in your 150.

Dunbar emphasizes that this group includes people whom you would feel comfortable joining *uninvited* at a restaurant or gathering. These people would likely be on your Christmas card list and invited to your wedding. While you feel at ease with these people, to spend focused time with them, you probably have to set a time in your schedule; you have to make an "appointment." They aren't so close that you are *already* with them; they are just outside that norm.

The group of 500 people, sometimes called a "tribe," is the group that a lot of people *think* is their 150-person friend group, but in reality, they can't sustain them as friends in that way. The 500-person tribe is often the overflow of the 150-person friend group. You probably identify their faces but might struggle to recall their names. You observe their activities and posts on social media—you may know they recently went on a trip or something happened with their family—but you rarely comment on their posts. You like them as people and might "like" their social posts, but you don't often take time to step into their lives, at least not anymore.

Dunbar's number is a well-established concept among sociologists. But so what? What does this have to do with the way God made us? I believe Dunbar, operating from the science of sociology, has accurately delineated our God-given relational levels. Many of us can naturally recognize these same patterns in our own lives. So if God designed these "levels" of relational connection, does the Bible give us any clues about how to approach relationships? Yes. It does.

MOSES'S NUMBER

God chose Moses to lead the Israelites out of Egypt. After crossing the Red Sea, Moses led the people of Israel through the wilderness. But things did not go well for the people, and one of the challenges was that everyone—thousands and thousands of people—looked to Moses for direction and problem-solving. As Moses tried to help the people, the book of Exodus explains, "Moses took his seat to serve as judge for the people, and they stood around him from morning till evening" (Ex. 18:13). Moses's father-in-law, Jethro, asked why Moses worked all alone from morning till evening, and Moses answered, "Because the people come to me to seek God's will" (Ex. 18:15). With wisdom, Jethro replied by giving Moses some advice, something each of us needs to learn. Jethro said, "What you are doing is not good" (Ex. 18:17).

Moses tried to be the leader, judge, and answer person for all the people of Israel. He tried to do it all and to be everything the people needed. Notice that Jethro observed the toll this task was taking not only on Moses but also on the people too. Jethro said, "You and these people who come to you will only wear yourselves out. The work is too heavy for you; you cannot handle it alone" (Ex. 18:18). Did you notice what he said? *You* will be worn out. *They* will be worn out. This is too heavy for all of you. Jethro advised Moses how to identify leaders who could instruct groups of ten, fifty, a hundred, and a thousand (Ex. 18:21)— sound familiar? Dunbar and the sociologists would have loved documenting this case study.

I have led a team of people who reach out to our local high school for nearly twenty years. Last year, a large group of adults joined our team. An equally impressive collection of student leaders were added to our team as well. I realized quickly that our group would have to operate differently.

For many years my wife had made homemade dinners for all the leaders before our weekly outreach event. Now, with many new leaders and the expanding size of the program, we realized we didn't have the time, money, or space at the table for twenty-five people to eat a meal each week. In prior years, we took time every week to hear how each leader was doing and often spent time praying for each one. I discovered that with this larger group of leaders, if everyone took two or three minutes, sharing and prayer could take an hour. When we ran our weekly meeting, I was bombarded with so many questions and minicrises in the ten-minute window before our meeting that I wasn't functioning as a nice human being. By the end of the night, I was spent emotionally, physically, and spiritually.

I had become a relational bottleneck and, unfortunately, a pain in the neck to everyone around me. What I was able to do efficiently for many years with ten to fifteen people had now exceeded a clear threshold when that group grew to twenty-five people. As Moses did, I wore myself out and everyone else around me too. I was trying to supervise *too many* leaders directly.

Everyone loses when we don't recognize our limited capacity for relationships. Jethro concluded his advice by telling Moses that adding more leaders "will make your load lighter, because they will share it with you. . . . You will be able to stand the strain, and all these people will go home satisfied" (Ex. 18:22–23). Jethro's advice to Moses gives us a snapshot of one moment, illuminating the numerical thresholds of relationships. And as helpful as this is, does the Bible give us any examples of these dynamics beyond this one small instance? Again, yes. Fortunately, Jesus gave us an extended example of how we can select a few circles of friends.

JESUS'S NUMBER

Robert E. Coleman's book *The Master Plan of Evangelism* is a classic. Coleman surprises readers because, despite its title, this book isn't about the nuts and bolts of evangelism. It is a book about leadership, discipleship, and, I would argue, friendship.

The best two pages of *The Master Plan of Evangelism* describe how Jesus did it. Coleman explains that in Jesus's second year of ministry, he had to narrow his group to a "more manageable number."[2] This number became the twelve apostles (Luke 6:13–17; Mark 3:13–19). Jesus collected a larger group of disciples beyond the twelve too. He had so many disciples that they were described as a "large crowd" (Luke 6:17). Further, Jesus appointed a group of the "seventy-two" (or "seventy") (Luke 10:1–20).

Coleman observed, "We must acknowledge that there was a rapidly diminishing priority given to those outside the Twelve."[3] How would you feel if you were given "rapidly diminishing priority" by Jesus Christ?

We should not rush past how this would affect us emotionally. We are all human. Recognizing that you are lower priority to someone you admire can be heartbreaking and frustrating. Jesus's ministry embraced the limits of his human capacity for relationships, despite how this exclusion must have felt to him and to those around him. Even within the Twelve, Jesus appears to have given additional, focused attention to three people: Peter, James, and John. Further, among those three, Jesus gave unique attention to the apostle John.

Jesus prioritized his relationships in group sizes of one, three, twelve, and seventy-two. These groups are eerily close to Dunbar's numbers. If we factor in the key women who also followed Jesus faithfully, we might have numbers like one to two (Mary and John), five (Mary, John, Peter, James, and the other Mary), and fourteen (the previous five plus the nine other disciples). We need not force any direct correlation to Dunbar, but one must admit that the correlations exist.

Another dynamic of Jesus's ministry and investment in his disciples is that his time with them was limited to three years. The Gospels don't give us a model for being with people, in person, for more than three years. One exception exists, of course: Jesus's mother. Mary watched him be born and die with her own eyes and was with him until the end. Mary was, in Dunbar's categories, Jesus's Level 0. We also acknowledge that Jesus sent the Holy Spirit to live within the disciples, but that isn't something we can do for our friends when we leave. Jesus's three years with his disciples provides us an uncomfortable truth about our limited capacity for friendship: friendship is temporary. Jesus's earthly friendship with his disciples, up to his death, was temporary. Some of us have a few lifelong friends, but even those are temporary, at least on this side of eternity. All earthly friendships end, even as they did for Jesus and his circle, through his departure from this earth.

MY NUMBER

My emotions have swung wildly over the years because of my failure to acknowledge how God made us incapable of maintaining endless close friendships. At times I have felt like a complete failure and have been tempted to give up. When I look back and think of the hundreds of people who were previously close friends, people with whom I shared significant parts of our lives together and have now lost any contact with, I feel like a fake. I feel like I made a commitment to them that I couldn't maintain. I feel like I lied to them. When I hear, every so often, that some of them are struggling in their lives, my ears hear a quiet whisper: "It is *your* fault. *You* didn't keep in touch." Someone call my counselor! Trust me, I know there are a lot of layers to my guilt; yet escaping one of these layers simply requires me to think differently, to think properly about my relational capacities.

Conversely, when I hear that some of my past friends are doing well in their lives, I hear a different whisper: "It is because you *didn't* keep in touch, they found *someone else* to invest in them that finally made the difference you failed to make." Ouch. On most days I'm strong enough to recognize that these messages aren't true. But not every day. We all need a better way forward to know how to select circles of friends based on our God-given limited human capacity for friendships.

HOW TO SELECT CIRCLES OF FRIENDS

God created you in such a way that you can select only a few circles of friends. What do you do with this truth? You can decide to do nothing, of course. But I'm going to guess that many of you reading this long for deep friendships. In light of what you can learn from Dunbar, Moses, Jesus, and people like me who seem determined to learn the hard way, I urge you to be *selective*, *shrewd*, and *strategic* in your friendships.

BE SELECTIVE

Our choice of friends must be selective. We select a limited number of friends because we must be realistic about our God-given, finite capacity for friendships. Pull out a piece of paper and write down who is in each of your circles of friends. Who is the one, or possibly two, person in your Level 0? Who is in your "sympathy group" of five people? Who are your "squad" of fifteen people? Who are your close friends in the group of fifty? These are difficult choices. This might feel as awkward as the elementary school question of naming your best friend. Do you know what else is difficult and awkward? Overpromising and underdelivering on friendship, especially to those closest to you.

When I completed this assignment and wrote down the names of people on my list, the first five to eight people were obvious. When I took the time to think through and rearrange the next dozen or so people, it was eye-opening. I realized I had been overlooking and undervaluing the people who were just a bit beyond my inner circle. Consider including these people in your speed-dial list or "favorites" list on your phone.

BE SHREWD (DISCERNING)

Our selection of friends must be shrewd. When I use the word *shrewd*, don't misunderstand it as a synonym for *rude*. Shrewdness is the intersection of being alert and intelligent. Being shrewd in relationships is the awareness, often in the moment, to make intelligent and discerning decisions about friendship.

I was with a wise friend of mine yesterday who shared with me a difficult relational decision she had to make quickly. She was recently on a trip with her son and his wife, who live in a different state and are in a busy stage of life. My friend looks forward to these rare and special moments with her adult children. Shortly before their three-day trip, my friend received the shocking news that a dear young person she knew had died unexpectedly and that the funeral would fall during the middle of her trip with her son and his family.

Let me make this clear: there is no playbook about how to respond correctly in these situations. What *is* required is wisdom and discernment.

What made this situation more difficult was that my friend quickly had to decide how to respond. She made a heart-wrenching decision, a choice that was made more difficult because of her immense compassion for others. She based her decision on the proximity of her relationships. She decided to prioritize the meaningful and infrequent trip with her son and daughter-in-law instead of attending the funeral. Did she make the right decision? I think so, but no one knows for sure besides her and God. We must admit that this situation, and many others like it, was complicated and multilayered. What I do know is that she exemplified in-the-moment awareness of her finite capacity for relationships.

The task of shrewdness in our friendships does not require instant and absolute prioritization of inner-circle friendships above all others. Jesus often prioritized complete strangers above his inner circle. But overall, *Jesus prioritized his time and attention to those closest to him.* This is why shrewdness requires us to be alert *and* intelligent. We need to think carefully about our friendships; in many cases, this requires thinking about long-term commitments and careful stewardship of our finite relational capacity. We must also notice what is happening right in front of our eyes. We need to be alert. We can't lock our gaze on the distant horizon so much that we miss the person right in front of us. Recall that Jesus was on his way to heal Jairus's daughter when he stopped everything to be with the woman who was bleeding (Mark 5:21–34).

So how can we be shrewd in our friendships? First, we must be familiar with the names on the list from earlier and know where each name falls in relation to the others. I know where my son stands on my list in relation to an old friend from high school. Second, we must ask God to make us alert to the people we encounter every day, whether they are on that list or not.

Third, in the midst of an urgent relational situation, we should routinely prioritize our inner circle before other people. That should be the trend, but a trend with exceptions. Again, this is what we see in the life of Jesus.

BE STRATEGIC

Our selection of friends should be strategic. We must be relationally strategic with our finite capacities of time, emotion, and commitment. God created us with limited personal resources in these areas, and we must steward them accordingly.

I learned long ago that "time management" is an oxymoron. We cannot manage time; we can manage only ourselves. Time keeps ticking—you can't manage the hands on a clock. We must, therefore, be strategic about how we manage ourselves with regard to time.

For me, this means that I preplan time with those who mean the most to me. Most of these people still live in my house. Many of these relationships are organic and happen conveniently; yet I still plan time with them. Proximity is not synonymous with connection. My wife and I work to keep a date night on our calendar. My children and I have weekly and annual activities that help us spend focused time together. In certain seasons of life, I put reminders on my calendar to call my closest friends, especially those who live far away. I usually plan these calls during regularly scheduled driving time. Some friends know I might call on Tuesdays or Thursdays on the way to classes I teach each semester. These plans help me fight the relational tyranny of the urgent.

EMOTIONAL-RELATIONAL CAPACITY

I teach and lead discussions on the topic of dating since I work with a lot of teenagers and college-aged students. Inevitably, I am asked about healthy physical boundaries in dating relationships. What most people don't ask about, but I always add to these discussions, is the importance of healthy emotional boundaries in dating relationships. I don't think it is wise to share too much physical affection with someone too early in a relationship, or to do so completely before marriage. I think it is equally unwise to share emotionally too much too soon with someone else. We should also avoid the opposite emotional extreme of being closed off and fearful. The best path forward is to be strategic about how and with whom we share ourselves emotionally.

Strategically managing our emotional capacity is not an easy task. But the same principle used to manage our time applies here. We routinely need to prioritize sharing emotionally with our inner circle before other people. For me, this means that I talk to my wife about important and emotional topics before I talk to others about these issues. It is not uncommon for my conversations with Erin to end with discussing boundaries about other people with whom I might chat about whatever it was we were discussing. I might say, "I think I might talk to Chris or Andrew about that; what do you think?" I am able to do this because I have taken time to think about where my existing relationships fit in my circles of friends.

One of the main challenges of friendship is that our commitment level changes over time. Someone who was once a close friend might now be a distant friend. I have learned to let go of trying to maintain my commitment level to my friends. I used to feel guilty about this. Now I feel that letting go of friendships is a confession of faith. I recognize that God made me incapable of maintaining deep friendships with everyone forever. I also occasionally tell people that I want them to be a more significant part of my life. As trite as it might sound, we need to face the reality of when our friendships are becoming closer or more distant.

One nuance of this commitment level is that relational reciprocity doesn't always apply. It might be that you are still the go-to person for someone else, though they are no longer that person for you. For instance, I have several mentors who are in my inner circle of friendship. I would call them immediately if I were in a tricky situation. But I'm not that person for them—they rarely call me for advice.

So how should we embrace our God-given, finite capacity and wisely select a few circles of friends? Select current friends who fit in each circle of friendship. Be shrewd to prioritize those who are closest to you while still being alert to those whom God puts in your daily life. Be strategic with your limited resources of time (look at your calendar), emotional energy (look at those with whom you already share heart-to-heart conversations), and commitment (acknowledge which friends are becoming closer and those who are drifting away).

FRIENDSHIP IN MAY 1995

In May 1995, in the wee hours of a Saturday morning, I exited a bus and waved goodbye to hundreds of people. As I walked to my car in the parking lot, it dawned on me: I would never see many of these people again.

Earlier that night, I sang, laughed, danced, and celebrated with hundreds of my fellow high school graduates. We enjoyed a well-planned night of fun called "project graduation," organized by the parents of the 1995 senior class of Arcadia High School. After walking across the stage, shaking the hand of our principal, receiving our diplomas, throwing our hats in the air, and taking photos with friends and family, we were whisked away in school buses for a long and late night set aside to celebrate safely.

Later, I realized there would be no more classes with these people, many of whom I had known since the second grade. Just like that, it was over.

The nature of our friendships showed that they were largely a function of proximity rather than connection. We mostly happened to be in the same place at the same time for many years. We knew each other's names, had shared a handful of personal details and memories, and some of our paths and levels of trust had ebbed and flowed closer and further away from year to year and month to month.

Time quickly showed that my friendships with the 207 other people in my graduating class were created almost entirely based on circumstance. When circumstances changed, through graduation, the friendships were shown for what they were.

Three months later I walked into the engineering commons of Arizona State University for my first day of college. I sat in a room full of new faces. My circumstances had changed. I learned new names, went to Aquabats and Black Eyed Sceva concerts, and had the courage to play basketball on the "A" court at the main gym. A few years and a graduation ceremony later, the names and faces changed again.

I don't know why it took me almost twenty years of attending high school graduations to teach me what I already should have known from my own life experience: I have to let go of friendships. Each of us can hold on to only a few friendships we acquire over time, and adding to these usually comes at the expense of other ones.

My friendships in 1995 lacked one major feature that has revolutionized modern friendships: social media. We must remind ourselves that the smiling faces of friends in an Instagram post hide the difficult work and initiative it takes to maintain a friendship off-screen. The sheer amount of data we have about other people today transforms how we relate to one another. I can hardly keep up with all the online data about my own family, and these are the people closest to me. Not only must we embrace our limited capacity for relationships, we must also embrace our limited capacity for information. This is a limit we will examine next.

CHAPTER 6

THE THIRD LIMIT: INFORMATION

Apple released an iPhone update in 2018 that included a feature called "Screen Time." As with most iOS feature updates, I didn't notice it at first. I sort of wish I had never seen it. Screen Time calculates how much time your screen is powered on and what is viewed during that time. To my surprise, I learned that I had spent twenty hours the previous week looking at my phone. It seemed like a lot of time to spend staring at a screen, and I thought, "What if I had cut that time in half? How would my week have been different?"

Screen Time provides further details about which apps I use and additional tools to notify me of and limit my phone usage. I'm surprised Apple made this feature available to its users. Effectively, Apple provided their customers with information that should shock most of us into using their product less. Several internet posts blew up in the weeks following the release of this feature, discussing the business implications of Apple's decision to do this.

I decided to try an experiment. I work with teenagers and

college students, and when I was with some of these students, I would ask them to pull up Screen Time. Most of them had no idea it was on their phone. Then I would ask them to look at the data and tell me what they thought of it.

Reactions were mixed. One high-achieving, top-notch, college-aged friend was shocked and immediately turned off all his notifications. He set up limits as well, especially to restrict the time spent on his favorite game: Clash of Clans. One of my high school friends' eyes lit up when he saw that in the previous week he had spent more than *eighty hours* on his phone. But it was his response to learning this that surprised me. He was indifferent and didn't care. "That makes sense," he said. "Crazy, right?" And in addition to the eighty hours on his phone, he also spends a lot of time at home on other screens as an avid Xbox gamer and YouTube watcher. Dare I mention that many hours of each school day are now spent in front of computers too?

Sean Parker, Facebook's first president, said that the thought process behind the development of Facebook was an attempt to answer the question, "How do we consume as much of your time and conscious attention as possible?"[1] Guess what? They figured it out. I know you know what I'm talking about. Facebook and Instagram have us figured out. They won.

Cal Newport, author of *Digital Minimalism*, observed that extracting eyeball minutes is more valuable than extracting oil. Newport recognized that "people don't succumb to screens because they're lazy, but instead because billions of dollars make this outcome inevitable."[2] The world's richest companies have spent their expansive resources—the resources of *the richest companies in the world*—to trick you into looking at your screens as much as humanly possible. For one of my friends, that is eighty hours per week, or 47 percent of each twenty-four-hour day. When does he sleep? Not much. When I see him, he is looking at his phone and is noticeably tired.

Let's run a thought experiment. Let's presume that it was possible to look at your screens for twenty-four hours a day, every day. There would still be *more information that you wouldn't have time to consume.* Even with our enormous consumption rates of information, entertainment, and data, it is always partial information; *our consumption is always incomplete.* As we discussed earlier, data engineers have said information storage already exceeds what humans can consume. All of us are living life and making decisions based on partial information. We never possess 100 percent of the information about *any* topic. We live in partial ignorance on *every* topic, and this will always be true.

I cringe when I talk about living life and making decisions using selective and partial sources of information. I worry about what I'm overlooking. I struggle not only with FOMO (fear of missing out); I also worry about FOMI (fear of missing information). I worry further about the trustworthiness of the sources I have already chosen. There is no humanly possible way around this conundrum. All of us live our lives and make choices based on partial information. The choice that we *do have* is to determine *how* we select the topics and sources of information we want to shape our lives.

NETFLIX ENDLESS SCROLL

"We're spending billions of dollars and making every show in the world. Our goal is the endless scroll. By the time you reach the bottom of our menu, there's new shows at the top. And thus, the singularity will be achieved. How are we doing it? Simple. We buy everything."[3] This is how a recent *Saturday Night Live* skit lampooned the task of the "new show development department" at Netflix. The narrator concludes the skit by announcing, "It will take twelve human lifetimes to watch all of our content. So start watching now!"

We can get a good laugh at a skit like this. One well-known formula for comedy is "truth plus pain." It is true that Netflix has more content than a human can realistically consume. Many of us, myself included, can confess to how painful it is to realize that we passed a healthy threshold when entertainment consumption becomes sloth.

The executives at Netflix and countless other entertainment, information, and data providers preselect what we will consume through detailed analytics. My friends at Facebook recently figured out that I need a dog training video—and they were right. These executives think a lot about your time, resources, and capacities. *There is a good chance they think more about your choices than you do.* You simply react to the choices their algorithms make *for you.*

I want to take you into a meeting right now.

In this meeting, a team of executives are planning, actually replanning, how you consume information. The bottom line is not to elevate a stock price or increase a profit margin. The bottom line, the thing that matters, is to glorify God and enjoy God forever, to "seek first his kingdom and his righteousness" (Matt. 6:33), to love God, and to love your neighbor as yourself. *If this were your bottom line, what would this team create as a plan for your information consumption?*

The team leading this meeting now has a plan they want to pitch to you. Let me walk you through six sources of information for you to preselect. These six sources create a hierarchy of inputs for you to consider.

INFORMATION SOURCE #1: BIBLE

Facebook successfully deployed their half trillion–dollar empire aimed at consuming as much of your time and attention as possible. Christian, how is that working for you?

I advise, instead, that you start deploying a ten-dollar tool to consume as much of your time and attention as possible: a Bible. You probably already have one.

How is your "Page Time" with the Bible? How would increasing your time with the Bible change your life? The Bible, of course, isn't the only source that can direct you to the topics and information that matter for Christians, but I'm certain every Christian would benefit from further focus on and study of the Bible.

I'm not here to guilt you into reading the Bible. The flourishing Christian life does not require you to sit at a table before dawn as you sustain a thirty-minute quiet time each morning. I know this for certain. How do I know? Because this type of study wasn't possible for the first fifteen hundred years of the church. Common people did not have Bibles; they were too expensive, not to mention that they were not available in the common language of those who were fortunate enough to know how to read. I'm certain God enabled people to flourish in their worship and relationship with him prior to when personal copies of Bibles became easily accessible to all believers.

Things are different today. Bibles are now readily available for most believers in their own languages.

My belief is that we should make the most of whatever resources God has made available to us. If you can read, use your ability to read the Bible. If you have money, you should buy a Bible. If you don't have money for a Bible, ask a church and they will give you one—or contact me; I'll get you one. If you can't read, listen to the free audio versions of the Bible online or on Bible apps.

I urge you to make the Bible the *first* source that you select to feed your limited capacity for information. Consider the benefits of engaging God's Word:

Keep this Book of the Law always on your lips; meditate on it day and night, so that you may be careful to do everything written in it. Then you will be prosperous and successful. (Joshua 1:8)

Your word is a lamp for my feet,
a light on my path. (Ps. 119:105)

Everything that was written in the past was written to teach us, so that through the endurance taught in the Scriptures and the encouragement they provide we might have hope. (Rom. 15:4)

All Scripture is God-breathed and is useful for teaching, rebuking, correcting and training in righteousness, so that the servant of God may be thoroughly equipped for every good work. (2 Tim. 3:16–17)

When we engage the Bible, we will prosper and succeed (Josh. 1:8), receive light for our path (Ps. 119:105), have hope (Rom. 15:4), and be equipped for every good work (2 Tim. 3:16–17).

Each year, I teach an introductory biblical interpretation class to three hundred brand-new, full-time ministry leaders. I give one assignment to complete in their first year of full-time ministry: to read the entire Bible. Most people read far more words per day than they realize—more on this below—but devote little of this capacity to reading the Bible.

My challenge might not work for everyone, but I'll challenge you too: would you consider reading the entire Bible in the next twelve months? If reading overwhelms you, would you listen to an audio version? Many useful reading plans are available online or in phone apps if you need some help.

In 2018 the largest Protestant Christian denomination in the United States released the results of their major survey of Christian growth. They determined that the leading factor in the maturity of a Christian disciple is Bible engagement.[4] I can't think of any better way to utilize your limited capacity for information and knowledge than to prioritize regular engagement with the Bible.

INFORMATION SOURCE #2: CHURCH AND CHRISTIANS WHO ACTUALLY KNOW YOU

Parenting is difficult. After nine months of physical, emotional, relational, and financial adjustments, most parents are already worn out before they get to the "starting line" of parenting. When our son Caleb was born, my wife and I were confronted with many in-the-moment tasks we knew were coming but for which we still were not prepared: swaddling, feeding, diaper changing, and safely installing the baby seat, just to name a few. The following years brought new challenges and chapters that often left us feeling like we were winging it every day.

Like many parents, my wife and I read many books, magazines, and information online about parenting. Not only did we feel like we wanted to be prepared and responsible parents, but we were also often simply desperate for solutions. Each day, we consumed an enormous amount of information about parenting. The information was helpful, but the best—and some of the most dangerous parenting advice we received—was from other parents.

God sent us the miracle we needed when we moved to Forty-Seventh Street. The miracle's name was Amy. We moved into our house with a one-year-old son and another child on the way. We did not know Todd and Amy from across the street when we moved there, but we did know they had little ones. When you are up at three o'clock in the morning with your crying child and you can hear another child crying across the street, you quickly become kindred spirits with your neighbors.

As great as Amy is, she is not a pediatrician, a nutritional expert, or a child psychologist. But Amy has a heart of gold, a generous spirit, a listening ear, and a heart for others and the Lord. No book, blog, or magazine could offer what Amy and her husband, Todd, provided us in those early years. We still read books and listened to experts, but Amy helped us fit those pieces of information into our actual lives.

You can google answers to parenting questions, of course, but truth be told, actual humans who know you can be one of the best resources for parents. At the same time, actual people you know can also be the most hurtful sources of input.

Two words will help you understand why: unsolicited advice. I quickly found out that you must be invited to give parenting input—even among close friends. In my naivete, I thought that my close friends who were parents would appreciate my telling them how they might be able to parent better. I was wrong. Really, *really* wrong. I was shocked to learn that some of my close friends would rather abide by the parenting advice of a blogger or writer whom they would never know than that of close friends who often prayed with them. After learning my lesson the hard way, I waited for the open doors of parental-advice invitations, many of which never came. I decided, instead, to make it my own habit to invite people I trusted and loved to speak into my parenting.

I share my personal parenting experience to illustrate a point about how the church can seek to be a source of information for people today, many of whom are not open to someone telling them how to live their lives. Remember, the church is not the building down the street, the church is *people*, Christian people. And when I say that the church should be a top source of information for how we live, what I mean is that we should regularly turn to other Christians for help, advice, and wisdom in making decisions.

Sadly, some people today think of the church primarily as a building operated by a pastor, someone they may or may not know personally. If that is your way of thinking, you are missing out on the true depth and richness of what God created the church to be. You are missing its strategic contribution to your limited capacity for information. While a church should gather every week and be led by a pastor, the true power of the church is the *people*, not the building or the pastor who preaches.

A pastor's input into your life is only one source of

informational nourishment available. Pastors have a tough job, especially in larger churches. It is quite common for a pastor not to know everyone in their church personally. So expect your pastor to organize excellent worship gatherings that include preaching, sacraments, prayer, and praise. But that isn't enough; we need more. And for that "more," we need other people—other Christians who are seeking to follow Jesus.

What you need is an Amy, or several Amys. We need input from *fellow Christians who know what we are going through.* We need to find others who live near us who have hearts of gold, generous spirits, listening ears, and hearts for others and the Lord. In the previous chapter, we explored our limited capacity for friendship. The fact is that you need a few Amys and Todds in your inner circle of friendship.

To embrace our limited capacity for information, we must commit to a local church and identify people we will get to know personally. But I want you to consider one more task as well. You need to *ask* for help. You might find that wise people in your church community are those who don't give uninvited input. Ask for help when life brings chaos. Ask for help, too, when life is humming along just fine. Asking for help, input, wisdom, and ideas catalyzes friendship, and it also catalyzes the life of the church.

INFORMATION SOURCE #3: PRAYER

If you were to go down the street from my neighborhood, you would find a surprise hidden among the endless rows of houses. Inside a large nondescript property, surrounded by a brick-wall fence, is a desert garden tended by nuns—a prayer garden. The

Evangelical Sisterhood of Mary is an organization of Lutheran nuns that has been committed to prayer, personal and communal repentance, and service since 1947. These nuns work mostly in the background and stay out of the way so visitors can enjoy a place of solitude and prayer.

You might wonder why I am suggesting prayer as a top source of information for our lives. How can prayer be a "source"? I'll explain why below, but I know from my own life that every trip I take to the prayer garden teaches me something I needed to learn. Prayer is a learning experience.

Prayer is an act that recognizes our human limits. There may be no better way to embrace our human limitations than turning to God in prayer. When we pray, we lay aside our abilities, reducing their contribution to zero. I confess that I am most often driven to prayer when my situations exceed my capacities. When I'm not powerful enough to change my circumstances, I pray. When I don't know who to talk to, am not sure what to say, or am not sure how a friend would react to what I need to say, I pray. When I don't have enough information, wisdom, or details about a situation I'm facing, I pray. What was the last thing you prayed about? It was likely something that fell outside your human capacity. Prayer is proof of our limitations.

Prayer is a source of information because when we pray, we process our lives with God. In prayer, we find our words. In prayer, we verbally process in a posture of recognition regarding the truth that we are human and God is God. It is in this process that we learn through prayer, and in this learning, we receive something from God that we did not have prior to our prayers.

I encourage you to embrace prayer as a recognition of your limited capacity for information. Psalms are a great place to start.

Consider reading a line from a psalm and then pausing for a moment, perhaps slightly longer than your gut tells you. Dwell there.

Try praying Psalm 139:23–24 right now:

> Search me, God, and know my heart;
>> test me and know my anxious thoughts.
>> [pause]
> See if there is any offensive way in me,
>> and lead me in the way everlasting. [pause]

If you tried this exercise, thank you. Did you learn anything? Do you feel like this experience was a high-quality source of information for your life?

Try praying Psalm 105:1–3 right now:

> Give praise to the LORD, proclaim his name;
>> [pause]
>> make known among the nations what he has
>>> done. [pause]
> Sing to him, sing praise to him; [pause]
>> tell of all his wonderful acts. [pause]
> Glory in his holy name; [pause]
>> let the hearts of those who seek the LORD
>>> rejoice. [pause]

Prayer teaches us how to think in the presence of God. The psalmists are great guides to the foot of the throne. The apostle Paul is another great guide for us. He wrote many prayers that can guide us. Consider his prayer for the church at Rome (Rom. 15:13):

> May the God of hope [pause]
>> fill you with [pause]
>> all joy [pause]
>> and peace [pause]
>> as you trust in him, [pause]
>> so that you may overflow with hope [pause]
>> by the power of the Holy Spirit. [pause]

When you pray Scripture slowly, let it hang in silence, and dwell in the moment, you upgrade the limited amount of data you can squeeze into your thoughts. Your brain and heart are a limited capacity hard drive. Delete useless files and replace them.

Jesus gave us the most important prayer to embrace (Matt. 6:9–13):

> This, then, is how you should pray:

>> "Our Father in heaven,
>> hallowed be your name,
>> your kingdom come,
>> your will be done,
>>> on earth as it is in heaven.
>> Give us today our daily bread.
>> And forgive us our debts,
>>> as we also have forgiven our debtors.
>> And lead us not into temptation,
>>> but deliver us from the evil one."

When we pray, we learn. Embrace prayer as a key input for your limited capacity for knowledge.

INFORMATION SOURCE #4: NATURE

Shooting stars do not confirm God's existence. But some students told me that a shooting star convinced them that God was real. It was my fault.

When I speak at camps, I often send students into the starry night to talk to God. And, yes, many of them tend to interpret a shooting star as a sign from heaven. I'm not against signs from heaven. Matthew's account of the birth of Jesus explains how a star guided the magi to Jesus. But a cloudy night does not negate God's existence. God is not in the business of "stars on demand." But he does use nature to speak to us; God uses nature to inform us.

We have taken a long look at our God-designed capacities as human beings. More specifically, we recognize that God created humans with capacities that are limited. We have made careful observations about the creational intentions of God. I want us to recognize that God also created everything else in the universe too; we do not exist in isolation. The opening chapters of Genesis show us that we are only a *part* of God's good creation. Just as God created you and me to have limitations, so too he made creation itself to have capacities and purpose. The capacities of creation, unlike human beings, are not created in the image and likeness of God. Yet the Lord has much to teach us through creation.

Stars or no stars, it shouldn't surprise us that God uses the night sky to teach and inform people about his existence. This is exactly what Psalm 19:1–4 teaches us:

> The heavens declare the glory of God;
>> the skies proclaim the work of his hands.
> Day after day they pour forth speech;

> night after night they reveal knowledge.
> They have no speech, they use no words;
>   no sound is heard from them.
> Yet their voice goes out into all the earth,
>   their words to the ends of the world.
> In the heavens God has pitched a tent for the sun.

Marketing teams and social media magnates meet in board-rooms, conspiring to consume as much of your attention and limited informational capacity as possible. Meanwhile, over the heads of all the people in the world, the sun rises and falls without fail. This is just one of the Lord's orchestrated events, designed to pour forth speech and reveal the knowledge of the glory of God for you to consume. Which one will you choose?

As you think about your information consumption, make nature a part of your intake. Go outside and take a walk. If you are an early riser, watch the sun come up. If you are a night owl, look up at the stars. I have found that the five-minute walk to our mailbox without my phone—I simply leave it in the house—helps me to recenter and refresh in a way that goes beyond the well-known physiological and psychological benefits. For me, these short walks are a minor effort of spiritual discipline. They are an acknowledgment that I need to stop what I'm doing and listen.

In his teaching on the important, complicated, and common issue of worry, Jesus recommends for people to "look at the birds of the air" (Matt. 6:26). One reason God created birds was to teach us a lesson about worry and anxiety. You could almost call them "therapy birds." God designed birds as a source of infor-mation for our lives. My advice is to make sure that you include nature in your limited informational diet. Go outside. Look out a window. Put a plant in your room. Get an animal, or maybe just a small goldfish. You will learn from these.

INFORMATION SOURCE #5: BOOKS

The average American spent sixteen minutes per day reading a book in 2018.[5] Meanwhile, Americans spent 144 minutes per day on social media.[6] Americans have a nine-to-one ratio of social media to book information in their lives. I urge you to consider reading more books. But not just any books.

The number of books released each year has recently eclipsed one million titles, many of which are released due to technological improvements in self-publishing. This means that readers of books have more titles than ever to choose from. Personally, I like that there are more choices, but this also creates a problem of quality.

As we think about embracing our God-given, limited capacity for information in terms of books, I want us to think about the quality of the books we read. Some books serve a short-term purpose, such as an entertaining novel or a book on Microsoft Windows 3.1, which was high-quality information in 1992 but is now useless information. Short-term-purpose books have their place. But I urge you to choose high-quality books. There is one easy way to identify a high-quality book: see if its popularity lasts. The older the book, the better chance that it is a high-quality book.

New books aren't inherently bad. They could be great. Only time will tell. The benefit of increasing our diet of older books is that we know they have stood the test of time. Will the bestselling book of last year still be in print in ten, twenty, or one hundred years? We don't know. But we do know that people continue to read older fiction such as Tolkien's *Lord of the Rings* and Steinbeck's *East of Eden* and nonfiction titles such as Augustine's *Confessions* and Anne Frank's *The Diary of a Young Girl*. Anyone who reads one of those books will know they are spending their time wisely. But there is an even better book.

The most important book you can read is the Bible. We already discussed this above, but it never hurts to say it again. Have you read all The Lord of the Rings books? Have you read the entire Harry Potter series? Have you read the entire Bible? *The Lord of the Rings* plus *The Hobbit* (*The Hobbit*, *The Fellowship of the Ring*, *The Two Towers*, and *The Return of the King*) totals 576,459 words. The New Testament, New American Standard Bible (NASB) translation, totals 184,590 words.[7] The Lord of the Rings books are over three times as long as the New Testament. *The Fellowship of the Ring* is longer than the New Testament. Harry Potter fans, don't hate me, but the Harry Potter series totals 1,084,170 words, and the entire Bible (Old and New Testament, NASB) totals 807,361 words.[8]

In brief, to embrace our limited capacity for information, read your Bible, read old books, and then, when you have done that, read books that serve a short-term purpose.

INFORMATION SOURCE #6: SCREENS

In 2017 the global market for screens was valued at $115 billion. This is expected to almost double by 2025.[9] Nearly 150 square miles of the leading types of screens are predicted to be produced per year by 2025. This is an area roughly the size of the city of Detroit—and that is for only one year.

I have taught theology and Bible classes at a university for over a decade. The feedback I receive from students directly, from the university in surveys, and from the netherworld of internet sites devoted to commenting about professors—yes, I looked—is that I'm a good teacher, I'm nice, and that I'm a strict grader. Students come to my class knowing that I carefully read their assignments and give constructive feedback.

I know that my students need assistance finding high-quality sources for their assignments. I can tell you that it is incredibly easy to identify when a student has built their essay around a simple Google search. Because of this, in my introductory lecture on research methods, I always say that Google (or Wikipedia) is an okay place to *start* but a bad place to *end*. I don't really want students to start with an online search. My classes are theology and Bible classes; this entire chapter could be a primer on how to prioritize research for most of the topics I cover in my classes. But I know students will eventually look online for information.

At this point in my life, I can't imagine living or working without screens. The real issue is *how* I will use them. Since we have a limited capacity for information, we must use screens wisely.

Here's the bad news: we don't use screens wisely. Not only do we spend 144 minutes per day on social media, but another study showed that in 2018 the average adult in America spent over 195 minutes per day staring at the screen on their phone, and that number is certainly increasing.[10] As I mentioned at the beginning of this chapter, a teenager I know shared with me that he had spent over eighty hours in the past week on his phone—that is over 685 minutes *per day*. No matter what we are doing on our phones, we are giving them too much time.

Here's the good news: we *can* use our screens wisely. I think it is unrealistic in our modern age to end our screen usage. Many fantastic books have been written about wise screen habits. Two excellent examples are Andy Crouch's *The Tech-Wise Family* and Cal Newport's *Digital Minimalism*.

In any given day, I might use my smartphone to access a Bible verse, text a friend I wouldn't otherwise talk to and receive prayer and fellowship from, or participate in conferences or lectures where the speaker wisely incorporates technology such as polls, quizzes, and Q&A features. While I believe that face-to-face education has many strengths, I am thankful that distance learning makes education available to students who might not otherwise be able to participate.

No matter what we do, we can't know everything. We can't know everything that exists; we can't even know everything we might want to know. Only God is omniscient; God is all-knowing. Humans are semi-knowing. Because of this limitation, we must preselect the sources of information that will help us be the people we want to be. *If we don't preselect the sources of information that we want to let form us, they will be preselected for us.* Profit margins will preselect for us. Corporate marketing teams are efficient and successful; they know what they want you to think about. I beg you to turn the tables and choose information for yourself.

What are you reading in the Bible? With whom are you spending time? Are you praying (and listening)? Have you gone outside recently or stared out a window? Can you find a time-tested old book to read? Are you mindful of how you consume the screens that surround you? Turn these questions into statements that reflect your preselection.

CHAPTER 7

LIMITED BUT NOT ALONE: GOD'S PRESENCE

If you were standing in the town center of Salisbury, England, in 1386, you could have heard a bell ring out over the countryside for the first time. You would have heard the Salisbury Cathedral clock. This clock had no dial, but it could strike a bell, if calibrated correctly, with a two-minute margin of error.

The Salisbury Cathedral clock was rediscovered in 1929 and restored to its original condition. Two large stones, hung from pulleys, drive its mechanism. The stones are wound up once a day to reset it, much like hand-winding a mechanical clock. This clock is one of the earliest known working mechanical clocks in the world.

Ancient Egyptians and Sumerians devised ways to keep track of time over four thousand years ago. Throughout the millennia, clockmakers, formally known as horologists (that's the

Latin term for people who are interested in the study and measurement of time), devised new methods to improve timekeeping. Water poured through holes in bowls and created water clocks. Candles of consistent size and substance were observed for their rate of melting to mark the time. Sand poured through hourglasses to establish consistent time measurement. The shadow of the sun on a sundial helped people estimate the hour on a sunny day. This required recalibration as the seasons changed, wasn't as useful on a cloudy day, and was useless at night. In the last thousand years, timekeeping has improved significantly as gears and weights, like those in the Salisbury Cathedral clock, were invented. Accuracy increased significantly through the use of pendulums and springs. Electronics were combined with the vibrational frequencies of quartz crystals and put into watches.

Today the International Atomic Time establishes the modern-era formal standard for accurate international time. International Atomic Time is the weighted average of over four hundred atomic clocks that reside in over fifty laboratories around the world. In June 2019 NASA launched the Deep Space Atomic Clock into outer space. This clock drifts no more than one nanosecond in ten days. What does this mean practically? It means that NASA has engineered a new clock that drifts one second every twenty-seven thousand years. I think that will do just fine for me.

Accomplishments in the human quest for precise timekeeping are impressive. Yet scientists admit that their best attempts are still not fully accurate. Scientists keep expanding the limits of accurate timekeeping but admit that they will never achieve it fully.

In the preceding chapters, we explored how God designed humans to have limited capacities. I argued that we are not

God; no matter how hard we try, we will never have the same capacities as God. God is all-powerful, or omnipotent; we aren't all-powerful—we are semi-potent. God is all-present, or omnipresent; we aren't all-present—we are semi-present. God is all-knowing, or omniscient; we aren't all-knowing—we are semi-scient. Not only have I worked to convince you of these truths, but I have also urged you to embrace these truths and have given you some practical ways to engage them wisely. In doing all this, I took a massive risk. Did you catch it?

I have built an argument that could lead me to be accused of deism. What is deism? I'll tell you.

Deism is a worldview in which a higher power created a universe infused with orderly laws that operate on their own without assistance. One simplified metaphor for deism is to view God as the "divine watchmaker." God—or the higher power or infinite architect—is the divine watchmaker who conceived of and created the universe. After it's conception, God wound up the universe like winding a clock, then walked away from it and let it operate on its own. Deism makes sense of our world in a naturalistic way that grants some supernatural design at the beginning but no supernatural intervention thereafter.

If you stopped reading this book after the last chapter, you might agree with me that humans have limits and that no matter how hard we try to improve our efficiency, productivity, and output, we, like horologists, will never achieve what we want. You could assume I am saying that we simply, like deists, need to recognize and work within our watchmaker's design without expecting anything new to happen. You might conclude that I am saying that we are here on earth with certain equipment and we simply need to recognize and accept its limits—end of story. The thing is, *that is not the full story*. The watchmaker *is still involved* with the watch and still intervenes powerfully in its operation and maintenance. In the final two chapters of this book, we will finish the story. In short, we are limited but not alone. God is present.

HEARING FOOTSTEPS

When we open the Bible, we see that every page describes God's activity. God is everywhere at all times. The psalmist cries out rhetorically, "Where can I go from your Spirit? Where can I flee from your presence?" (Ps. 139:7). The answer is self-evident. We are unable to flee from God's presence; God is always near. Abraham Kuyper put it this way: "There is not a square inch in the whole domain of our human existence over which Christ, who is Sovereign over all, does not cry, Mine!"[1] God has always existed and has always been immanent in our reality, whether we recognize it or not.

God communicates with us, always. God speaks to us through the very existence of light and dark, land and sea, stars and space, animals and bugs, and, perhaps most of all, other people. Creation is the evidence of a creator; it is the "always on" indicator that God is engaged and active in interacting with us. God chose to speak before any ears existed. Genesis 1:3 states, "And God said, 'Let there be light.'" God *spoke* before any created thing could hear. God's communication began within the Trinity before anyone else was listening. God speaks even when he knows that no one will hear him besides himself.

God kept communicating (the Bible states that "God said"

in Genesis 1:3, 6, 9, 11, 14, 20, and 24) as he created water, land, plants, stars, animals, and bugs. God's voice filled the grand auditorium of his creation. It isn't until Genesis 1:26 that God creates humans, and finally, in 1:28, we read, "God blessed them and said *to them* . . ." (emphasis added). The sound waves of God's voice finally fell upon human ears for the first time. I hope they were listening.

God communicated with humans in two ways throughout the first two chapters of Genesis. He spoke through the materials he created out of nothing (e.g. stars, earth, plants, animals), each of which begs the question "Why is *this* here?" or, better yet, "*Who* made this?" The second way God communicated was through his own voice. But when we turn to Genesis 3, we see that he took a radical and unusual third step in interacting with humans: God walked with them.

In Genesis 3:8 we read that Adam and Eve "heard the sound of the Lord God as he was walking in the garden." Follow the progression here: first, God communicates through his creation; second, he communicates through his voice; third, he communicates by his presence among his people. God did not set up the universe and then, like the deistic concept of the watchmaker, walk away from it. From the first pages of the Bible, we see that God's presence is active among his creation and his people.

A RIVER FLOWING IN A TENT

At two o'clock in the morning, I realized that our situation was getting worse and that I needed to do something. A small but growing stream emerged and was running right between my wife's sleeping bag and mine. The small trickle of rain that had begun at eight o'clock had turned into a torrential downpour. I can sleep through almost anything, but I couldn't continue sleeping through this. As much as I tried to ignore the situation, I had to wipe my eyes, peek my head out of my cozy and warm mummy-style sleeping bag, and survey what was going on. My wife and three children had been awake all night. The inflatable cushion my daughter was sleeping on was now floating like a pool toy in the emerging pond inside our tent. I had to do something.

Fortunately, our trusty Honda Odyssey wasn't far away. I rushed my family into the safe confines of our suburban chariot. Meanwhile, for the next hour, I accelerated my campsite cleanup as each strike of lightning approached. I didn't bother wearing my rain jacket; the rain thoroughly soaked me within a minute.

I'll never forget my family staring through fogged-up windows as I packed up our tent and everything else with it. After thirty minutes, I had shoved all our stuff into the back of our van and found out the Odyssey could effectively double as a mud-romping, forest-road-traversing escape vehicle.

I didn't grow up camping. Fortunately for my family, I learned how to camp and set up a tent when my college buddies and I started frequenting a place we called "The Spot" at the Mogollon Rim near Payson, Arizona. I found the routine of setting up the tent, entering its warmth and safety each night, and taking down the tent the next day to be a bit of a treasured ceremony. For me, the tent provided an escape, an adventure, and a memorable time of community.

After God "showed up" through the sound of footsteps in the garden of Eden, he made himself known in many ways to his people, but the most significant and obvious next interaction was a surprising one. God's presence emerged on earth uniquely and tangibly inside an unusual object.

Around the fourteenth century BC, God told Moses to lead the Israelites out of Egypt. Next, God told Moses to go up Mount Sinai and there gave him the Ten Commandments. After a bit of a false start, Moses communicated God's instructions to the Israelites, and part of God's directions to Moses included a command to build an unusual object: a tent.

This tent, also called the tabernacle, became a place where God spoke with Moses "face to face" (Ex. 33:11). In turn, Moses acted as God's spokesperson before the people (Ex. 35). God is not a tent; he met with Moses *within* the tent. The difference is important. A mysterious tension to God's presence in the tabernacle allows us to say at the same time, "God is everywhere (omnipresent)," and then point to the center of the tabernacle and say, "God is *there* in a special and unique way."

The tabernacle provided the people of Israel a constant reminder of the Lord being in their presence. The presence of God means good news for God's people! While the people themselves were created with limited capacities, the tabernacle reminded them that their unlimited Lord was present among them.

Though their ancestors had been kicked out of the garden of Eden, where God *walked among them*, Israel now had opportunities to re-enter the location of God's presence on earth. Better yet, through the gate of repentance and sacrifice, drawing near to God is possible. Comfort is palpable as sweet-smelling incense fills the air, and the tent moves everywhere with the people of Israel (or rather, the people followed the cloud above the tent wherever it went, see Num. 9:17). The tabernacle communicated that God chose to *dwell* among his people, his limited and sinful people.

GOD GETS AN ADDRESS

Erin and I moved four times in the first four years of our marriage. Upon returning from our honeymoon, we drove north from Phoenix, Arizona, to Spokane, Washington. When we arrived, we learned, for the first time, how to drive in snow, wear fleece often, and endure cloudy days.

After two wonderful years, we packed up everything we owned and drove south to Cave Creek, Arizona. We unpacked as much as we could into the small guest house of a generous friend and left the rest of our unpacked boxes in his garage. A few months later, we loaded up our belongings again, drove about thirty minutes south, unpacked and moved into our very own two-bedroom apartment.

A little more than a year later, with a small but growing family, we needed to move again. This time we found a house that was literally on the other side of our apartment's backyard wall. This decision made moving easy. We walked our stuff over to the wall and dumped it over into our new backyard. We were tired of moving and hoped to settle down. We remained in that house for the next three years before moving again. We have been in our current home for over ten years, and that has been, well, much nicer. It wasn't until we had stayed for a while that we put a cute little rock near our front door that said "The McGevers." We had finally found our home and felt settled.

Many people like camping for a few days. If you are brave, you might stay for a week or two. But you are unlikely to find someone who has willingly camped in a tent for months or even years. It appears that King David felt a little guilty living in the comfortable confines of a house while the Lord's dwelling place was the tabernacle. David said as much to the prophet Nathan: "'Here I am, living in a house of cedar, while the ark of the covenant of the LORD is under a tent.' Nathan replied to David, 'Whatever you have in mind, do it, for God is with you'" (1 Chron. 17:1–2). God didn't allow David to build the temple, but his son, Solomon, oversaw its construction. The temple was built to create a permanent house for the ark of the covenant and, in turn, a lasting dwelling place for the presence of God on earth.

The temple attracted chaos over the subsequent centuries. King Hezekiah peeled gold off the doors and doorposts to pay off foreigners (2 Kings 18). The temple was eventually destroyed and burned by Nebuchadnezzar in 587 BC.

It was during this time that prophet Ezekiel explained, "Then the glory of the LORD departed from over the threshold of the temple and stopped above the cherubim. While I watched, the cherubim spread their wings and rose from the ground, and as they went, the wheels went with them. They stopped at the entrance of the east gate of the LORD's house, and the glory of the God of Israel was above them" (Ezek. 10:18–19). The Spirit of God had departed and no longer dwelled in the temple.

Israel rebuilt Solomon's Temple in the time of Nehemiah and Ezra (ca. 515 BC). The temple was later defaced and converted into a temple of Zeus in 167 BC. It was not until 37 BC that the temple was restored. Herod the Great significantly upgraded the temple (beyond Solomon's design) in size and grandeur to appease the Jews of that era. This is the temple of the New Testament era. But one thing never returned to the temple. Nowhere do we read that God chose to dwell there again. Instead, God decided to reside on earth in a very different way. God came to earth as a man.

WE ARE NOT ALONE: GOD BECAME FLESH

God's special presence on earth shifted to a better temple. The gospel of John announces, "The Word became flesh and made his dwelling among us. We have seen his glory, the glory of the one and only Son, who came from the Father, full of grace and truth" (John 1:14). Jesus, the second member of the Trinity, dwelled among us. The underlying Greek word for "dwelling" is from the verb "to tabernacle" or "to tent." John purposely used this language to let the reader know that God's presence united with human flesh in the same way it had filled the tabernacle. The result was that people saw God's "glory" in Jesus Christ—the same glory that previously appeared to Moses on Mount Sinai (Ex. 24:16–17; 33:17–23) and that also filled and departed from the temple. The next chapter of John makes this claim explicit: "Jesus answered them, 'Destroy this temple, and I will raise it again in three days.' They replied, 'It has taken forty-six years to build this temple, and you are going to raise it in three days?' But the temple he had spoken of was his body" (John 2:19–21).

In chapter 2, "Humans Are *like* God?" we explored the two natures of Jesus Christ; Jesus is fully God and fully human. When God became man, God displayed his special presence not in the sound of footsteps, not in a mysterious location above the ark of the covenant, but united to human flesh in the person of Jesus Christ. Paul explains that Jesus "made himself nothing by taking the very nature of a servant, being made in human likeness" (Phil. 2:7). Jesus's earthly ministry demonstrated God's special presence on earth. But that ministry didn't last forever.

Shortly before his ascension, Jesus commanded his followers

to go and make disciples of all nations. While some disciples still doubted (Matt. 28:17), I'm certain that some of them (likely including Peter) were eager to get started. But many Christians overlook what Jesus told them to do first. Jesus told them to wait (Acts 1:4). Wait for what? Jesus told them to wait for "the gift my Father promised. . . . You will be baptized with the Holy Spirit" (Acts 1:4–5). Shortly after Jesus said this, Jesus ascended into heaven (Acts 1:9–11).

CHRISTIANS ARE LIMITED BUT NEVER ALONE

Jesus, fully God and fully human, told his fully human friends to wait for the baptism of the Holy Spirit. That was because Jesus gave his limited human followers and friends a nearly unlimited task: to disciple the entire world. Jesus told them to wait—to stop first, to not even attempt to move forward at all—until they were first filled with the Spirit of God. God wanted to empower his followers to participate in omni-God-sized tasks in limited-human ways. This participation would require the fundamental change of them being filled with the Holy Spirit. Theologians sometimes call this mingling of our limited human capacity with God's unlimited nature "union with Christ."

Union with Christ has at least two components. First, it brings the declaration of the forgiveness of our sins. Second, it provides us the gift of new life. John Calvin said that in union with Christ, believers are "participants not only in all his benefits but also in himself"[2] and that "day by day, [Christ] grows more and more into one body with us, until he becomes completely one with us."[3] Theologian J. Todd Billings commented on Calvin's statement, saying, "This union is always empowered by the Spirit, for by this Spirit we 'come into participation in God.'"[4]

Jesus told his disciples to wait for the baptism of the Holy Spirit because he wanted to equip and empower them to carry out the task of worldwide discipleship—a massive task beyond human ability. Jesus did not want them to attempt to do what was humanly impossible.

Even though Jesus was fully God and fully human in every way, the presence of Jesus on earth was "among" but not yet "in" humans (John 1:14). Jesus said his going away would be to our advantage: "Unless I go away, the Advocate will not come to you; but if I go, I will send him to you" (John 16:7). But why? How is it better if Jesus leaves us? Again, the answer is found in the gift of the Holy Spirit. After telling his disciples to wait, Jesus said, "You will receive power when the Holy Spirit comes on you; and you will be my witnesses in Jerusalem, and in all Judea and Samaria, and to the ends of the earth" (Acts 1:8).

Pentecost is the breakthrough moment when God's promises are realized. The work of Jesus had a purpose. Yes, to forgive our sins. But why? *To restore us to God, that we might live with God and walk with him yet again.* And that is why the Spirit is the fulfillment of Jesus's work—the mystery of the ages, Christ dwelling in us through the Spirit. Pentecost is the climax of God's plan to bring the kingdom of God from heaven to earth. And God's plan for today, until Jesus returns, is to do this work through *you.* You are still limited, but you are not alone.

Finite humans are filled and united with the infinite God to do his work on earth. Paul asked rhetorically, "Don't you know that you yourselves are God's temple and that God's Spirit dwells in your midst?" (1 Cor. 3:16). The process of union with Christ and being filled with the Spirit is both immediate and progressive. We immediately gain the presence of God within us and benefit from the merits of Christ for our forgiveness. We also progressively grow and experience our participation in the kingdom and life of God over time.

We have seen that every human is limited. No one can be physically present in two places at once, no one will ever know everything, and no one will run a one-second mile. These limitations apply to all humans. While Christians are limited just like every other human, we are also different: the Spirit of God lives inside us.

Your capacities as a Christian always remain *human*. You do not become all-present, all-knowing, or all-powerful; you continue to be semi-present, semi-knowing, and semi-powerful. But through the power of the Holy Spirit, you are united to God in a powerful way that provides new and fresh directions for you when you reach your human limits. When you reach the end of your rope, when you run into the dead ends of your human capacities, the indwelling of the Holy Spirit provides you ways to move forward.

FOMO

In 1986 I watched a movie titled *An American Tail*, an animated musical adventure about a mouse and his family as they emigrate from Ukraine to the United States. I don't remember much about the movie, but I do remember the title song, "Somewhere Out There," by Linda Ronstadt and James Ingram. The song won two Grammy Awards and had a music video I'll never forget. It begins with Ronstadt singing alone while looking out her window at the moon. In the next scene, Ingram is elsewhere but also looking out his window looking at the same moon. The video climaxes at the end with the two of them coming together.

I saw this movie when I was ten years old, and as a child of the 1980s, I frequently watched the music video on MTV. In that season of my life I was alone a lot. As I mentioned, I'm an only child with a single mom who worked extra shifts to put food on the table, and I resonated deeply with the idea of being all alone and looking out at the moon and thinking that someone else, perhaps even my mom during the short moments of her break as a waitress at the restaurant, was looking up at the same moon. The song gave me hope that I wasn't alone—even though I was.

As Christians, we have an even better reason to hope and can know we are not alone. Christians are in union with Christ through the power of the Holy Spirit. When the Holy Spirit indwells us, we have access to God in a new and fresh way. While I can't be present with loved ones who are in different places because I am bound to only one location, God is not bound by that same restriction. God is omnipresent. And because I am in union with Christ through the power of the Holy Spirit, and since the Father, Son, and Spirit are present everywhere, this means I am connected with the God who is present with my loved ones, wherever they might be. We see Paul leaning into this concept in his letter to the church in Corinth: "Even though I am not physically present, I am with you in spirit. As one who is present with you in this way . . . when you are assembled . . . I am with you in spirit, and the power of our Lord Jesus is present" (1 Cor. 5:3–4).

Paul wasn't physically present in Corinth when he wrote

his letter, yet he said that he was with them "in spirit." New Testament scholar Gordon Fee explains that Paul meant more than simply "you are in my thoughts." Instead, Paul "understood himself to be present 'in spirit/Spirit' in [Corinth]."[5] The reason Fee uses the upper and lowercase S in the quote is because both senses of "in spirit" are available to the Christian. The first sense—of a general human sensibility—is available to every person, similar to the idea that you are in my thoughts. The second sense, the sense represented by the capital S, relates to the Holy Spirit and applies to Christians specifically since they are indwelled with the Holy Spirit. This is not an isolated idea in Paul's thinking. He makes a similar argument to the Colossian church in Colossians 2:5: "Though I am absent from you in body, I am present with you in spirit."

As a parent of three teenagers, I think this secondary sense of spiritual presence—the unity we have in the Holy Spirit—is especially important. My wife and I wish we could be with our children in person as much as possible, but the seasons of our lives and theirs are changing. I have a fear of missing out (FOMO) on my children's life experiences, and that can be painful and heart-wrenching at times. The truth is that I can't be everywhere, or with everyone I want to be with. I'm limited just like every other person. But as a Christian, as a person indwelled by the Holy Spirit, God has given me a way to channel these longings to be with others and care for people from afar. As Christians, we can do more than look out our windows at the moon and think nice thoughts about those we love. Through our union with Christ and the power of the Holy Spirit, we are united with an omnipotent God who is everywhere and with everyone at all times.

FOMI

When I was a child I thought parking lots were scary places, and for some reason grocery stores were the worst. Grocery store parking lots are full of cars pulling in and out of parking spaces while people are walking close to the parked cars in each row. The drivers pulling out struggle to see the people walking by, and random grocery carts add to the chaos. If a ballot proposed that grocery-cart pushing required a license, I'd vote for it—especially for the Costco parking lot. People walking in and out of the store tend to be looking at their lists, phones, and receipts, never at the cars whizzing by. As a child, I thought the parking lot felt like a real-life version of the video game Frogger, where you guide a frog across a busy street and a pond of dangerous obstacles. Fortunately, my mom was always there to hold my hand and safely guide me into the store.

Earlier we learned that humans can't know everything. We are always semi-knowledgeable about every topic, even the ones we're interested in, and that is one of our limits. When we become Christians, our human nature does not magically change. Keanu Reeves's character Neo in the movie *The Matrix* may have been able to instantaneously download dozens of martial arts styles into his brain and proclaim, "I know kung fu," but that isn't how human beings learn, and that limit doesn't change when you become a Christian.

While Christians don't gain special information or secret knowledge, we do gain a guide, a guide who is within us, operating from the inside out. Jesus made an initial promise to his disciples in John 14:26: "The Advocate, the Holy Spirit, whom the Father will send in my name, will teach you all things and will remind you of everything I have said to you." This is one reason why Christians believe the writings of Jesus's apostles are inspired by the Holy Spirt and a reliable guide for our lives. The apostle John also wrote to a broader group of Christians: "The anointing you received from him remains in you. . . . His anointing teaches you about all things and as that anointing is real, not counterfeit—just as it has taught you, remain in him" (1 John 2:27). When John wrote of the "anointing" that "remains in you," he was describing the Holy Spirit.

A frequent word for the Holy Spirit in John's writings is the word *paraclete*. *Paraclete* is a Greek word that is translated as "advocate," "counselor," or "helper." All these concepts are roughly similar to the notion of a "guide," and none of them imply that the Holy Spirit is a spiritual "fact book." The difference between a guide and a fact book is obvious. A guide is relational, open to conversation and able to adapt to the nuances of different situations, applying in-the-moment wisdom and insight. A fact book, on the other hand, can't do any of this. It simply records facts as fixed statements. This is one reason why our union with Christ through the power of the Holy Spirit changes us as human beings. We never come to know everything we *could* know about God, life, people, or most anything, but the indwelling of the Holy Spirit *does* guide us through everything we need regarding God, life, people—and everything we need for eternal life, for that matter!

Now that I'm tall enough to see above and around the cars and have experienced years of close calls, I'm a savvy parking lot navigator. When my kids were little and I wanted to teach them parking lot safety, I did not hand them a children's book titled "How to Survive the Parking Lot." Even if they managed to read the book, there is no way the book could cover every possible scenario they would encounter. Similar to my FOMO (fear of missing out) on the life experiences of my children, as a parent, I also have a perpetual fear of missing information (FOMI) in what I teach them. I want them to be well-prepared and equipped with the right information to make good decisions. So what did I do? I made sure they held my hand tightly as we threaded our way across the perilous path of the parking lot. And that's a great picture of how God guides us in our spiritual growth. As limited humans who are indwelled by the Holy Spirit, we seek to hear God in Scripture and to trust and obey God as we follow what he says.

FOMP

When God doesn't answer my prayers, it's hard—probably one of the most challenging recurring experiences of my Christian life. Not only is it incredibly frustrating, it makes me mad, sad, and frustrated to the point of yelling and crying at times. I like to be in control and don't enjoy situations where I'm not in control. I think of the time my friend Troy died despite a massive community of earnest Christians praying for his healing. And times like this are all the harder when I read the experiences of the Spirit-filled believers in the book of Acts who seemed to experience more direct answers to prayers than I typically see in my life. At the same time, I am aware that God did not design human beings to have unlimited power. I am not omnipotent, so even in prayer, I remain dependent on God to move and act. We never force God's hand.

The limits of human power and ability are obvious. We can't run a one-second mile, we can't jump over a mountain, and we can't heal our loved-one's sickness by wishing it. Similar to our fear of missing out and our fear of missing information, each of us has a third fear: the fear of missing power (FOMP). Yet again, as Christians, we are united through the power of the Holy Spirit to the omnipotent God of the universe that has the power to do all things.

The indwelling of the Holy Spirit provides us with internal power to change our hearts and minds and fill us with love and knowledge. Consider Paul's words to the church in Ephesus:

> I keep asking that the God of our Lord Jesus Christ, the glorious Father, may give you the Spirit of wisdom and revelation, so that you may know him better. I pray that the eyes of your heart may be enlightened in order that you may know the hope to which he has called you, the riches of his glorious inheritance in his holy people, and his incomparably great power for us who believe. That power is the same as the mighty strength he exerted when he raised Christ from the dead and seated him at his right hand in the heavenly realms. (Eph. 1:17–20)

> I pray that out of his glorious riches he may strengthen you with power through his Spirit in your inner being, so that Christ may dwell in your hearts through faith. And I pray that you, being rooted and established in love, may have power, together with all the Lord's holy people, to grasp how wide and long and high and deep is the love of Christ, and to know this love that surpasses knowledge—that you may be filled to the measure of all the fullness of God.

Now to him who is able to do immeasurably more than all we ask or imagine, according to his power that is at work within us, to him be glory in the church and in Christ Jesus throughout all generations, for ever and ever! Amen. (Eph. 3:16–21)

God the Father, through the Spirit, can give us "wisdom and revelation" so that our "heart may be enlightened" and we may "know the hope to which he has called you." Further, we can be "strengthened" with power "in your inner being" and enabled to grasp "love that surpasses knowledge." Notice that Paul highlights the reality of God's "power that is at work within us." When Christians gain wisdom, revelation, hope, strength, and love that surpasses knowledge, these are real and identifiable artifacts of his power at work within us. Yet the Spirit's power is not limited to only an internal work in us. Wait, there's more.

The indwelling of the Holy Spirit also provides access to external power for situations beyond our control. There is a spectrum of beliefs here among Christian believers. On one end of the spectrum is the belief that Christians have no influence at all in the universe. We simply accept what happens as the will of God and seek to live faithfully with the cards we are dealt. On the other end of the spectrum is the belief that Christians have full influence over the universe. If we have faith, we can accomplish anything. Neither of these views, as extremes, are true. As with most things in life, the truth is somewhere in the middle. We know God is able to do "immeasurably more than all we ask or imagine according to his power that is at work within us" (Eph. 3:20). So on one hand, God, at times, will do *more* than we ask or imagine. This does not mean we are the ones with the power to accomplish this work; it is possible only because of "*his* power that is at work *within us*" (emphasis added). On the other hand, we know that many of our prayers aren't answered, perhaps because our requests aren't aligned with the mysterious will of God. Paul addresses our lack of knowledge in his letter to the church in Rome: "The Spirit helps us in our weakness. We do not know what we ought to pray for, but the Spirit himself intercedes for us through wordless groans. And he who searches our hearts knows the mind of the Spirit, because the Spirit intercedes for God's people in accordance with the will of God" (Rom. 8:26–27).

Throughout the Scriptures, Paul highlights human weakness as an opportunity to magnify God's power. When we feel weak, prayer is one way to "access" God's power. And even when we feel we can't do that well, the Holy Spirit intercedes on our behalf and prays for us according to God's will.

A few years ago, I was asked to speak at the weekly chapel at Grand Canyon University, where I work. Full confession: I was intimidated. Grand Canyon University holds chapel in a seven-thousand-seat basketball arena, and usually most of the seats are full. Fortunately, the staff asked me to do this several months prior to the event, so I spent a lot of time thinking about what I might say. I paid special attention to the themes and issues going on in the lives of my students on campus. The key moment in my preparation came when I walked out of my class one afternoon and into the arena. It was a normal Tuesday. The arena was empty and had some, but not all, of the lights on. I went about halfway up the stands and sat where the students would sit when I led chapel. I asked God to give me a word to share with them and got down on my knees on the sticky arena aisle in front of a folding seat and tried to listen to God as best I could. I sensed that the students who would be coming to chapel were overwhelmed with their academic lives, their personal lives, and their spiritual lives, and I knew one thing for sure: as I walked out of the arena, I knew I didn't want to give them one more thing to do. I chose Romans 8:26–27 as my Scripture text for chapel because I wanted the students to know that the all-powerful Spirit of God continually intercedes on their behalf. I wanted them to know that though their power might be, and likely was, depleted, God's power through the Spirit is sufficient and able to do immeasurably more than they could ask or imagine.

Every one of us has limited capacities. God designed us with these inherent limitations, and they remain even when we are restored in right relationship with God. But something does change when we have that relationship. We now live our lives in unity—in union—with God, an ongoing relationship where through our dependence and trust we are able to do more together with God than we could ever do on our own. Human capacities and abilities, though limited, are still quite amazing. But when our limited capacities are united with God's power, that's when miracles happen.

We aren't deists who, at best, endlessly seek to maximize our human capacities for the good of the world. Christians have within them the Spirit of the living God and are portable tabernacles of the Holy Spirit. We are *not* God, but in union with God, we are empowered because Christ now lives in us through his Holy Spirit.

As great as that is, we're still not at the end of the story. There is more. Because even though human capacities are miraculously multiplied through the power of God's Spirit, who is able to do more than we can, God created us with still greater potential. And that potential is fully realized only when Christians, united with God, work in collaboration with other believers. The collaborative capacities of human beings are amazing, shocking, and downright scary. We will explore this in the next chapter.

CHAPTER 8

LIMITED BUT NOT ALONE: THE CHURCH

Talk show host Stephen Colbert called it "the first place I go when I'm looking for some knowledge . . . or when I want to create some."[1] Singer Sufjan Stevens said, "It's kind of beautiful—it's all the product of imagination; it's not reality at all."[2] Matt Mullenweg, the creator of WordPress, said that using it creates "lots and lots of small contributions that bubble up to something that's meaningful." Perhaps the best comment about it is what Michael Scott, the fictional regional manager from the TV show *The Office*, said. He called it "the best thing ever."[3] What is it?

Wikipedia.

On January 15, 2001, Jimmy Wales and Larry Sanger created the first edit to Wikipedia. When I checked today, I found that Wikipedia is the eighth most visited website in the world. The English edition alone includes over six million articles. Authors add or edit over 8 words per second.[4] Wikipedia's goal is to "compile the sum of all human knowledge."[5]

The best wide-ranging compilation of information prior to Wikipedia was the *Encyclopedia Britannica*. *Britannica* was first published in 1768 in three volumes. Editors chose recognized experts to write articles on preselected topics. The editorial staff then checked the accuracy of the articles and compiled them into printed volumes. In 1933 this encyclopedia adopted a continual revision schedule to improve and update articles regularly. Sales of the volumes reached their height in 1990, in which 120,000 sets were sold. After that, demand dropped significantly. In 2010 the company chose to print only twelve thousand copies. Only four thousand copies sold that year. On March 14, 2012, Encyclopedia Britannica, Inc. announced it would no longer publish printed editions; they moved their efforts online. Their consistent effort at compiling knowledge over the past 244 years had been disrupted.

In the past, when people needed quick information about a topic about which they knew too little, they often searched for an encyclopedia. This required finding a physical copy at a library, school, or, if you were lucky (printed encyclopedias were not cheap), in your home. If you opened an encyclopedia, you were likely to find information on the topic you were interested in, but not always. The information might be dated, too specific, too general, exhibit implicit or explicit bias, or fall prey to other issues. In 2005 the BBC reported that twelve-year-old Lucian George read each of the thirty-two volumes of the *Encyclopedia Britannica* and located several significant errors. His research revealed, for example, inaccuracies about the location of bison in Europe. His discovery prompted the editors of *Britannica* to initiate a project to rewrite their article on the country of Poland to be included in their next printing.

Today when people need quick information about a topic they know little about, Wikipedia is often the first place they look. And they have to go no further than their smartphones. It is free. It is updated constantly. It is available in 312 languages.

No one claims Wikipedia is perfect. In 2006 the article on the famous, and very alive, English soccer player David Beckham insisted that he was a Chinese goalkeeper in the eighteenth century. Wikipedia is liable to all the weaknesses of the *Encyclopedia Britannica*. It can, however, be corrected immediately and secured to a certain extent through its editorial hierarchy. Further, the number, length, and detail of the articles are seemingly endless.

If you have been alive for more than a few decades, I have a question for you. Did you ever consider writing an article in an encyclopedia? Probably not. Most of us don't have the experience, education, and reputation to contribute what we know on the limited set of important articles printed in an encyclopedia. The final printed version of the *Encyclopedia Britannica* included fewer than five thousand contributors. I wasn't one of them. You probably weren't either.

I have another question for you. Could you contribute *something* valuable to Wikipedia? The answer is certainly yes. No one has the same combination of experience, interests, and insight as you. You might not be a likely contributor to an article on the history of the Statue of Liberty. But, for example, my seventeen-year-old son is an expert on the rugby players at Pinnacle High

School in 2019; he is a world expert on this topic. He has information that no one else in the world has.

Wikipedia provides a way to accumulate the collective information of as many humans as possible. Wikipedia is a project that presses the limits of the human capacity for information. This was all possible because of one concept: collaboration.

COLLABORATION GONE WRONG

I'm about to tell you a story about a collaboration that went terribly wrong. But first you need to know that the key to collaboration is communication. Communication is possible between humans because of five senses. Smell, touch, and even taste allow us to communicate. But the combination of sight and hearing forms the basis for the most powerful communication and collaboration tool available: language.

Wikipedia's engineers created a platform to bring together 312 languages to assemble multilingual collaborative information. Imagine what would happen if the language barrier were easier to navigate. Imagine if "the whole world had one language and a common speech." You don't need to imagine it—this is a direct quote from Genesis 11:1.

Genesis 11 follows the creation and fall narratives (Gen. 1–3) and several other prominent accounts of the outworking of sin in the world (for example, Cain murdering Abel, and God's judgment of the world through the flood). Genesis 10 is known as the "Table of Nations." This chapter describes the descendants and families of the sons of Noah and their geographic spread. Noah, like Adam, had been told to "be fruitful and increase in number and fill the earth" (Gen. 9:1, 7; see also Gen. 1:28) The command was clear: humans were to increase in number and spread out across the earth.

At first the people did what God told them. They were fulfilling the command to fill the earth as they journeyed east (Gen. 11:2). As soon as they came to the plain in Shinar, they settled and made plans for a permanent dwelling. This is when things began to go terribly wrong.

The people rejected God's original mandate for them to fill the earth. They instead started a different project, their *own* project, which required them to build a city with a tower to reach to the heavens. The aim of their building project was "so that we may make a name for ourselves; otherwise we will be scattered over the face of the whole earth" (Gen. 11:4). Rather than filling the earth as God instructed, they wanted to stay together and stay put. They wanted to make a name for themselves through a massive, collaborative project that could be seen from far away and even reach to God's heaven. The project did not hinge on the technology of bricks and mortar—technology is morally neutral. The irony is thick when, in Genesis 11:5, the Lord "came down" to see their city and tower. Even with the people's strong collective effort, the Lord "couldn't" see their work from above. The narrative is not calling God's omniscience or omnipotence into question; it is mocking the tininess of the tower compared with God. The gap between human capacity and divine transcendence is infinite because it is categorically different.

This gap is infinite, or in mathematical terms "undefined," like trying to divide a number by zero. But Genesis 11:6 hints at a difficult concept. It states, "If as one people speaking the same language they have begun to do this, then nothing they plan to do will be impossible for them." A deep and mysterious correlation exists between human collaboration and outcomes that are beyond what we can ask or imagine. The sin in Babel could be titled "The Power of Community Gone Wrong." There was nothing intrinsically wrong with their common language; the problem was their denial of their God-given purpose. Their refusal to participate in the greater mission of God and instead choosing to have their own mission and act independently was what led to their demise.

God intervened. God confused their language (Gen. 11:7) and scattered them all over the earth (11:8). The city of Babel was filled with "babblers," people who literally couldn't understand each other. God capped the power of human collaboration. They misused language, communication, and collaboration for a self-seeking purpose rather than for the mission God gave them.

FIVE ROBOT LIONS UNITE

I am a product of watching too much 1980s TV. On Saturday mornings, I woke up early and shuffled, sleepy-eyed and still in my pj's, to the kitchen. I grabbed a bowl, some Cheerios, a spoon, a few spoonfuls of sugar—this was before presweetened Honey Nut Cheerios were sent straight from heaven—poured some milk, and headed to the living room. I carefully adjusted the dials to minimize the static so that I could see the "crisp" picture of our new color TV. Then I waited for my favorite show to come on.

I watched all 124 episodes. Each show began with a deep-voiced narrator saying (imagine this in an ominous and dramatic tone), "From days of long ago, from uncharted regions of the universe, comes a legend. . . . This is the story of the super force of space explorers, specially trained and sent by the Alliance, to bring back Voltron, Defender of the Universe." Voltron was my fave.

Voltron was a Japanese-American animated series dubbed into English. The show chronicles the adventures of five pilots who control five robot lions that combine to form Voltron, Defender of the Universe. The plot of each episode was predictable, but I didn't care. Early in each of the episodes, each of the robot lions fought valiant battles.

Eventually, they faced a foe who was too difficult to overcome on their own, individually. And then, as if you weren't expecting it, something magical happened. The Black Lion formed the head and torso, the wings of which formed a powerful shield. The Red Lion formed a right arm with a blazing sword. The Green Lion was the left arm fitted with a powerful cannon. The Blue Lion was the right leg, and the Yellow Lion the left leg. They came together to form something greater than the sum of their parts; they formed Voltron, Defender of the Universe. Plot spoiler: they won every time. Episode over. Refill my bowl of Cheerios and add extra sugar.

SPIRIT-FILLED HUMANS UNITE

In the last chapter, we explored how God's special presence arrived in the footsteps of the garden, above the ark of the covenant in the tabernacle and then the temple before departing, in the person of Jesus Christ, and finally, in Spirit-filled Christians, beginning at Pentecost. Christians are God's temple, and God's Spirit dwells in them (1 Cor. 3:16).

At Pentecost, tongues of fire came to rest on each person, and each one was filled with the Holy Spirit (Acts 2:3–4). People often end the story there. When we do that, we miss God's vision for the church; we miss God's vision for our lives. We overlook God's plan for a better way forward in light of our limits.

When the day of Pentecost came, much of what had been done to scatter the people in Genesis 11, at Babel, came full circle. On this day in Jerusalem, the festival of Pentecost drew "God-fearing Jews from every nation under heaven" (Acts 2:5). These were the descendants whose ancestors were initially driven apart by the Lord at Babel. They filled the earth and were prepared to be reunited through the recent work of Christ. The crowd was bewildered because they heard voices in their own languages (2:6). God had confused their languages for his own purposes, and now the Spirit was allowing them to understand each other for the Lord's purposes.

Pentecost *reversed* Babel. Previously, at Babel, God dispersed the people for using their limited yet surprisingly powerful capacities of collaboration in disobedient, self-serving ways. Now, at Pentecost, people united to use their limited but newly Spirit-filled capacities within the community of the church to carry out God's mission on earth. The book of Acts provides a snapshot of what this community looks like. The book of Acts demonstrates *the collaborative power of limited humans united to an unlimited God*.

The early church shared their resources. They held all things in common (Acts 2:44). They gave their collective resources "to anyone who had need" (2:45). They met together, ate together, and were glad together (2:46). In this atmosphere of community and collaboration, the Lord daily added to the number of people being saved (2:47). As time went on, the early church continued to share their resources (4:32–37). As their Spirit-filled collaboration brought them together, they "were one in heart and mind" (4:32).

Many churches today, including wonderful ones I participate in, struggle to be of one heart and mind. We look more like dispersed Babel-ers than Pentecost-ers. We build self-serving artifices rather than the community-serving, community-resourcing, community-sharing, Spirt-led gospel communities that we read about in Acts. Consider Acts 4:33–34: "With great power the apostles continued to testify to the resurrection of the Lord Jesus. And God's grace was so powerfully at work in them all that there were no needy persons among them." Their collaborative *message* was the resurrection of the Lord Jesus. Their collaborative *action* was to provide for each other, especially those who were needy.

COLLABORATIVE PRACTICES IN THE EARLY CHURCH

We discussed that humans are designed with limited capacity to change circumstances. God is all-powerful; humans are not. I urged you to consider how you can commit to acts of faithfulness rather than expecting to accomplish things that are outside your capacities.

When the early church faced needs that exceeded God-given human capacities, we see the interweaving of human and divine capacities to meet the needs of the world and the church.

What we don't see is a directive for individual Christians to become superhuman. God does not change our inherent capacities when we are filled and united with God's Spirit. Christians and non-Christians are equally human. This is why blogs, books, and coaches for human productivity succeed and fail equally for Christians and non-Christians alike. Christians are limited in their God-given capacities, just like non-Christians. But Christians, unlike non-Christians, come into union with Christ through the indwelling of the Holy Spirit and can operate within the church alongside other Christians to contribute to God's purposes for the world in a way that exceeds human capacity.

I have lived and ministered in the same community for nearly twenty years. I am familiar with nearly every local church and pastor in our area. My community has a wide variety of strong and healthy churches, but at least one clear weakness exists among them: they rarely collaborate and communicate with each other. There have been glimmers of hope at times, such as when the Luis Palau crusade came to our city about a decade ago. That outside team pulled churches together to collaborate in a powerful way. I'll never forget sitting in a massive ballroom, surrounded by nearly every minister in our large city, for the kickoff planning event. It was exciting and inspiring. More recently, several initiatives in our community are working effectively to network churches and ministers together to share their ideas and resources and to be there for each other relationally. But if I'm honest, most churches I interact with operate fairly independently or only within their existing, closed networks. I know churches are meant to communicate and share with each other because that is what we see modeled in the early church, and Jesus taught about the power of united Christians. Sadly, if churches don't work together, they will have to work harder than they are designed to—and will accomplish less than their full, collaborative potential.

The early church collaborated with their limited resources. If a church needed additional leadership, another church sent people. If a church needed money, other churches took an offering and sent it. If a church lacked letters of the Bible, they circulated them. So there is clearly power in working together. But let's not think that collaboration itself is the secret. It takes collaboration and God's Spirit to accomplish God's purposes.

Just as you and I are limited in our individual capacities, our collective communities are limited too. The church, even a larger collaboration of churches, will always be limited in what it can accomplish because humans aren't omnipotent, omnipresent, or omniscient. And early in the Bible, we see a clear warning that there are dangers in thinking our collaboration—apart from God—will be the answer to our problems.

DECONSTRUCTING BABEL

In Genesis 11 we saw that the people of Babel had a desire to build something. They were united together with a clear goal: "Let us build ourselves a city, with a tower that reaches to the heavens, so that we may make a name for ourselves" (Gen. 11:4). But they did not stop with the aspirational goal of making a name for themselves; they recognized that this would need a specific, identifiable concrete goal. They literally tried to build a stairway to heaven.

And the people were willing to cooperate to accomplish their goal. The entire narrative of Babel utilizes plural pronouns: "*They* found a plain in Shinar and settled there. *They* said to each other, 'Come, *let's* make bricks and bake them thoroughly.' *They* used brick instead of stone, and tar for mortar. Then *they* said, 'Come, let *us* build *ourselves* a city, with a tower that reaches to the heavens, so that *we* may make a name for *ourselves*'" (Gen. 11:2–4, emphasis added). No individuals are named in the account of Babel. Who started this movement? Who was the first one to find the plain in Shinar? Who had the idea to bake bricks? Who thought up the tall tower? We don't know and it doesn't matter. The narrative makes clear that what matters is that they worked together.

The people in Shinar would not have been able to progress toward making a name for themselves unless they had the tools and resources for their goal. They baked bricks instead of utilizing stone and used tar for mortar (Gen. 11:3). The people in that area likely had no choice but to use bricks since stone wasn't readily available in that area, so they used the tools and resources that *were* available to them rather than focusing on what wasn't available.

Finally, we should note that the construction project in Shinar was not only a massive tower, the people built an entire city (Gen. 11:4). This city must have been a significant accomplishment since the Lord "came down to see the city and the tower the people were building" (Gen. 11:5). The people had much more than an idea, a cooperative approach, and a good collection of resources; they got started and put in the hard work of accomplishing the task *together*.

When the people of Shinar rallied around a clear goal, decided to cooperate, utilized their resources, and worked together, the outcome was so significant that the Lord proclaimed, "Nothing they plan to do will be impossible for them" (Gen. 11:6). The weight of this assessment is hard to fathom. The trajectory of their collaboration was so powerful that the Lord intervened by confusing their language and scattering them over all the earth. Clearly, there is power in human beings—even with our limited capacities—coming together around a common goal.

And despite the negative assessment we should make of Babel's building project, there are some lessons to be learned here—even from failed human efforts to cooperate together without God. In today's church many Christians are quick to rally around an aspirational goal of "glorifying God," but we often fail to identify how to get there. Hats off to the Babel builders—they had a clear goal in mind. And they worked together. Often I see Christian efforts that highlight individuals more than the collective power of their communities. Is it any surprise that these crumble under the weakness of our individual human limitations?

Thankfully, we don't need to look to Babel as the model for cooperation. Though they accomplished much by working together, Acts 2 shows us what is possible when human cooperation is joined with God's power. At Pentecost, God brought together scattered people with different languages and miraculously united them through the power of the Holy Spirit. The rest of the book of Acts shows how Christians rallied to be Jesus's witnesses (Acts 1:8) as they attempted to cooperate, share resources, and put in the hard work of limited individuals to collaborate in the massive effort of the church. Each of us is limited, but we are not alone, and just as God brought together Christians two thousand years ago to form the church, we can put those insights to work today in our churches and communities.

RECONSTRUCTING FOR A LIMITLESS CHURCH

Christians are united with Christ through the Holy Spirit to a God who has no limits. And the church is the collective assembly of people who are indwelled by the Holy Spirit. If the Lord can say about the people of Shinar, "Nothing they plan to do will be impossible for them" (Gen. 11:6), then how much more is this true for Christians who come together with God's Spirit indwelling them. So let's get practical.

First of all, the people of the church function best when there are clear goals. Clear goals usually arise when individuals agree that there are obvious or immediate needs. When the COVID-19 pandemic arrived, churches scrambled to find ways to connect with their members virtually. For many churches, an obvious and immediate need arose: the need to provide live video for church services. A friend of mine in a small town is a faithful parishioner of a humble community church. When he and his wife realized that they, and the rest of their community, were going to be stuck at home for the foreseeable future, he contacted the pastor and other church leaders. Together, they identified a clear goal of providing streaming services within two weeks. The goal was specific, and it reflected the desire of the entire community.

Goals function as mile markers for an overall vision. One of the strongest churches in my community has a vision to equip people to live and flourish as a disciple of Jesus. The church provides several "next steps" for individuals to take toward this vision, including discovering Jesus, being baptized, worshiping, and serving. Those steps are wonderful and powerful, but they are also primarily focused on the individual. To take their vision a step further, this church, like many churches, also establishes temporary and clear goals to meet immediate needs in their broader community. The church is currently aiming to train one hundred new leaders to serve the community and is renovating their facilities to make them more accessible for people of all ages, abilities, and backgrounds. Finally, they are partnering with Habitat for Humanity and other local churches to build one hundred homes in their area for under-resourced families. The church established these goals through discussions with its members, leaders, and several other churches who are aware of the needs of the community. When these goals are met or come to an end, the church plans to reassess and decide on the next set of goals. Here is the key, though. *None of these goals could be accomplished by one individual Christian; these goals are possible only through the collaborative power of the church.*

This example shows the importance of cooperation. Individuals will always be constrained by their own limitations. It is only when Christians cooperate with one another and learn their roles that they will exceed their limits.

I coached high school basketball for ten years, and the toughest part each year was the tryouts, and the most difficult part of tryouts were the cuts. You might assume that during tryouts I spent most of my time assessing each player as they dribbled, passed, and shot the basketball. That is what most players assumed, as was clear from their excitement after making a jump shot or beating a defender with a crossover move. Their belief was also obvious when they turned the ball over and yelled in frustration. But as a coach, I expect players to make and miss shots, and I realize they will make good passes and bad ones. What most players fail to realize is that one of the primary skills I look for is *what they do when they don't have the basketball.* At any given time, ten players are on the basketball court, and (usually) only one player has the ball. I observe how each athlete plays basketball for the 90 percent of the time the basketball isn't in his or her possession. Because only one out of ten players has the ball at any given moment, much of the success of the team depends on what players do when they don't have the ball. In basketball this means playing excellent defense, knowing the offensive cuts, setting picks, boxing out during rebounding, and more.

One of the hidden keys to successful cooperation in the church is what people do when they "don't have the basketball." Like my players, most people think of cooperation and see themselves as the one doing something, whether that is in the power position, making the decisions, or assisting with a big play. Usually they think of what they will do "with the ball." But in the church you rarely "have the ball," and cooperation is mostly how well you follow the lead of others. The Bible teaches that Christ is the head of the church (Eph. 1:22), so even "senior pastors" are called to cooperate primarily as followers rather than being at the "top" of their organizational charts—they aren't the "point guard" of their churches.

John the Baptist is an excellent example of the power of cooperation for the sake of God's plan for the world. When John's disciples alerted him that people were going to Jesus instead of John, he said, "He must become greater; I must become less" (John 3:30). John collaborated with Jesus's plan by humbling himself and recognizing his limited role. In an age when personal "brand building" and "platform" management are prioritized, we can take a cue from John the Baptist and learn what it means to cooperate with Jesus as he leads the church.

Another aspect of cooperation we need to think about is

utilization of our tools and resources. Each of us has limited power, presence, and information, but when we pool these resources, God uses them in ways we could never imagine.

I am a part of a network of ministers that meet to discuss the needs and dynamics of our community. Our community is large and growing, and one of the priorities of our network is to start new churches in our neighborhoods. This might seem surprising since there are already dozens of churches in our community, and to be honest, most of the churches would like to add more members to their own congregations rather than starting new churches. Yet we all recognize that on any given Sunday, there aren't enough seats in our existing churches for everyone in our community to worship. Further, we know that greater geographic reach and more denominational variety will help more people in our community find their place in a local church, so many of the churches in this network contribute toward starting new churches in our community. Last week I met with a pastor of a new church plant down the street from my house, and he told me that my church, as well as others, was contributing financially to help it get started. I wasn't surprised.

■ ■ ■

Do you know what a bass guitar sounds like? The bass is an interesting instrument. Some people can't quite pick out its sound when they are listening to a song because it tends to be low and rhythmic, sort of a background to the primary melody. This happened recently when I played my son a song with a great bass line (in case you are interested, it was "I Can't Quit You Baby" by Led Zeppelin). While my family and I were driving to dinner in our

Honda Odyssey, I played the song. While my son was loving the bass line, my daughters said they couldn't even hear it. They *could* hear Robert Plant's singing, Jimmy Page's piercing guitar, John Bonham's famous floor tom triplets, but they couldn't quite pick out John Paul Jones's intricate bass line.

Last Sunday our church had a simplified worship team that included people playing an acoustic guitar, piano, and drum set. Interestingly enough, while we all enjoyed the worship, one of my daughters said, "Dad, the music sounds like something is missing. It sounds hollow." I told them that the guitar and piano were carrying the high end of the music and the drum set provided the beat, but they were missing an instrument to fill out the low end, which normally comes from the bass. The limited, and often overlooked, contribution of the bass player magnifies the individual contributions of the rest of the band. To put it simply, they are all better when they come together.

Finally, let's talk about the value of plain old hard work. Existing together in community as a collection of disconnected individuals takes little or no effort, especially when only a few people do all the work (and they work at 150 percent to make up for the others). Truly collaborating and working together as a body requires a lot of work. Working independently may feel easier and even more efficient, but God designed limited-on-their-own humans to operate best when they collaborate.

■ ■ ■

Do you like ice cream? Then you might enjoy the collaboration between middle-school friends Ben Cohen and Jerry Greenfield, who came together to create Ben & Jerry's ice cream. Do you like computers? Then you are probably aware of the hard work of childhood friends Paul Allen and Bill Gates, cofounders of Microsoft. More of an iOS person? Then you can look to the partnership between Steve Wozniak and Steve Jobs. In a previous generation, if you were to walk into a pub in Oxford in the 1930s or 1940s, you might have noticed a group of writers discussing, criticizing, and reading one another's unfinished works. This group included, among others, J. R. R. Tolkien and C. S. Lewis. If you look into any of these partnerships, you will learn that each member was individually brilliant, personally driven, and likely would have been successful all on their own. Collaboration can be inefficient, especially at first, because it requires coordinating, stopping, listening, communicating, disagreeing, compromising, and much more—all of which can be hard work.

The way I imagine it, the tower of Babel was initially the brainchild of one person. The idea would never have taken off without that person sharing the idea with another person. There were likely disagreements about how to make bricks, how to stack them, and more. Yet they worked through these issues to the point where God came down from heaven and proclaimed, "Nothing they plan to do will be impossible for them" (Gen. 11:6). The people in the plain of Shinar discovered the advantages of working together rather than alone. But people indwelled by the Spirit of the living God have something they did not: the blessing of God's Spirit empowering God's work. We have yet to see the full potential of God's people working together in unity to accomplish God's purposes.

CHAPTER 9

STAYING IN OUR OWN LANE

I own a sparkling green bowling ball engraved with *Sean* right above the finger holes. I can't use it anymore because I got it when I was eight years old, so my fingers no longer fit in it. My mom bought it for me because she signed me up for a bowling league. Each week, I went bowling. No one told me what to do; I just imitated what I saw other people doing.

When I was learning to bowl, I started carefully. The ball was heavy. The floor seemed slippery. I didn't want to embarrass myself.

A few weeks later, I started throwing the ball harder and with more confidence. I was in a bowling league off and on for about a year. One of the things that happens to eight-year-olds is that they grow. I grew. My fingers grew too. The combination of my chunky fingers and energetic throws led to wild times at the bowling alley.

THE GOOD NEWS OF OUR LIMITS

I specialized in two variations of terrible throws. The first was when I would swing back so hard that my bowling ball did not roll down the lane. Instead, the ball popped off my fingers and flew backward toward the seats of those sitting behind me. The second specialty my chunky fingers perfected was when the ball would not release on time. The ball would be stuck on my fingers, continue on the upward arc of my arm swing in front of my body, and then release somewhere toward the ceiling. The ball arced through the air, fell heavily toward the delicate wooden lane, and echoed with a resounding thud throughout the entire bowling alley. Bowlers everywhere looked first at the implosion site of my sparkling, green "Sean" bowling ball, and then heads swiveled down the lane to spot me as I scurried to hide amid the ball return machines.

The only thing worse than a "sky" ball was when my ball flew diagonally through the air into the adjacent lane, landing in someone else's way, veering straight into their gutter, ruining their game and score. I learned the phrase *stay in your lane* as an eight-year-old because I frequently heard this phrase in my bowling league. I wanted to stay in my (bowling) lane, but sometimes I simply couldn't help myself—I struggled to stay in my lane. My neighbor's lane was not my lane.

One of the practical challenges of our collaboration in life and in the church is to stay in our lane. We must recognize the tasks God has given us and the gifts God gave us to accomplish them. Part of embracing our God-given limits is staying in our lane. The Corinthian church struggled to stay in their lane. Paul reminded the church that each person was given an assortment of gifts. Paul said, "There are different kinds of working, but in all of them and in everyone it is the same God at work" (1 Cor. 12:6). God worked differently through different people in the church to accomplish his work. Paul continued and said, "Just as a body, though one, has many parts, but all its many parts form one body, so it is with Christ" (1 Cor. 12:12). The Corinthian church struggled to make sense of this. They favored the gifts of some and minimized the gifts of others. This led to division in their church. Paul made it simple for them. He taught them that an ear does not make a good foot and an eye makes a poor hand.

Christians constitute the church, and the church is the body of Christ. Paul wrote, "You are the body of Christ, and each one of you is a part of it" (1 Cor. 12:27). The English language does a poor job with the second person plural; formally, we use the word *you* whether it refers to one or many people. Readers, especially American readers, of 1 Corinthians 12:27 can be tempted to think, "I am the church." Nothing could be further from the truth. Paul uses the plural *you* in this verse. We should read it like this: "Now *you [all]* are the body of Christ, and each one of you is a part of it" (emphasis added). Friends from the South could even substitute *y'all*. The church is a collaborative effort of a community of Christians. It operates best when each Christian stays in their lane to contribute their part. Don't try to do more. Don't be an eight-year-old bowler.

STOP, COLLABORATE, AND LISTEN

God designed each of us with limited capacities. When we enter union with Christ, we are filled with the Spirit of God to contribute toward the tasks of God. God gave us the church as the ultimate collaboration tool to make the most of our unique gifts for these tasks. How do we do that?

Stop. Each of us needs to do some serious introspection about our own personal limits and boundaries. We must reject the secular narrative that we can accomplish whatever we want if we put our minds to it. We must reject the false Christian narrative that we can do "all things" as Christians. We must stop and admit that the modern obsession with productivity and efficiency leads us to certain failure and idolatry. God gave his people a regular task that runs counter to the pervasive demands of our society and many of our churches: sabbath. Be realistic about what you can do in twenty-four hours. Be reasonable about what you can do in seven—no, six—days. We must stop thinking that we have God's power and capacity.

My advice to stop is largely advice about the way we *think* about ourselves; it is advice to think differently. I urge you to think biblically and theologically about the way God has intentionally made us as finite humans. I urge you to embrace God's design rather than the world's design for your life. After stopping and believing these truths, we must move beyond what we think and believe; we must act. One way to act on these beliefs is to collaborate.

Collaborate. Each of us must collaborate with the Spirit of God and with the people of God. Through the Spirit, we unite with Christ. Paul wrote, "I have been crucified with Christ and I no longer live, but Christ lives in me. The life I now live in the body, I live by faith in the Son of God, who loved me and gave himself for me" (Gal. 2:20). If you have faith in the Son of God, say to yourself now, "I no longer live, but Christ lives in me." You are not alone. You collaborate with *Christ in you.* Your capacities are limited by design. Christ's capacities are unlimited. Yield to God's ways.

The irony is that when we come to grips with our incapacity, we grow further in the grace and power of God. We join John the Baptist, who said, "He must become greater; I must become less" (John 3:30). We join Paul, who said, "I will boast all the more gladly about my weaknesses, so that Christ's power may rest on me" (2 Cor. 12:9). We should collaborate not only with the Spirit of God within us by declaring our incapacity but also with those who join us in this declaration. We must be engaged with other Christians in the church as a profession of our own incapacity.

Scripture is clear that we, as humans, are made in the image of the triune God and, being such, are designed by God to collaborate with the Spirit of God (through our union with Christ) and with other believers (the church). When we resist and reject our individualistic attempt to pursue the tasks of the world, our churches, or ourselves and instead stay in our lane, collaborating with God and others, we will be amazed at what is possible.

Listen. After we stop and recognize our own limits and work to collaborate with the Spirit of God and the church, we must continually reflect and listen. As we try to embrace the good news of our limits, we will fail. If culture doesn't bamboozle you, the Deceiver, Satan, will. The Serpent's lie first promised humans that they might be "like God" (Gen. 3:5). Satan continues to lie to us. Peter tells us to "be alert and of sober mind. Your enemy the devil prowls around like a roaring lion looking for someone to devour" (1 Peter 5:8).

When you fail, listen to your failures. Isolate the source of your failure. Were you trying to do too much? In your endeavor, were you driven by the Spirit of God or by the spirit of the world?

Can you identify fragments of your failure in which you, to put it bluntly, attempted to be "like God"? Listen to the source of your failure and recognize that Satan may have whispered in your ear, "You can, should, and must be able to do this . . ." Do not tiptoe around the fact that some of our aspirations are demonic because we don't want to *yield* to God, we want to *be* God.

One way to listen is simply to listen to your body.

Are you physically worn out? Ask yourself if you are attempting to live beyond your physical limits. Are you frequently tired because you don't get enough sleep? Does your body hurt? Are you often sick? While there may be health-related reasons for your body to be functioning poorly, have you considered that your belief system might be to blame? Consider going to a medical doctor, but also consider going to a pastor or a trusted Christian friend to discuss how your aspirations may be taking a toll on you.

Are you emotionally worn out? Ask yourself if you are carrying too much emotional weight that you now need to off-load onto others within the church. You also should ask yourself if you are emotionally "numbed out," meaning that you may have not stopped and listened to your emotions in the midst of your hustle.

Are you spiritually worn out? Ask yourself if you have been trying to be your own spiritual leader. Instead, ask for help. Humble yourself, and ask a Christian to mentor your spiritual life. You would also be wise to listen to those around you, taking time to hear from people in your inner circle. Ask them about your life balance and pace; ask them if you are attempting to push beyond the limits of what God has for you.

Listen to your life—it is speaking. Your life can be like an indicator on a car dashboard that warns you that you need to embrace a change in your life.

REIMAGINING "YOUR" LIMITS

When I was in college, a mentor of mine told me that people's one-year goals were too large and their ten-year goals were too small. So I did the obvious thing: I decided to set five-year goals. Since then my five-year goals have served me well. Now, I want to ask you: What are *your* dreams? What are *your* goals? What are *your* hopes? Do *your* God-given limits shape these goals? What role does the Holy Spirit play? How might the larger church community contribute to what God has put on your heart?

My encouragement to you is not to "limit" your goals, dreams, and aspirations, but instead to reimagine them in light of the way that God made you and every other human. The "good news of your limits" is great news because it provides operating instructions for you to live the way God designed you. There is a good chance that your short-term dreams are too big because they are constrained by your limits. There is also a good chance that your long-term dreams are too small because you have not considered how the Holy Spirit and the people of God play a part in what God wants to do through *you* collaborating with *them*.

I encourage you to take smaller and shorter ministeps of faithfulness within your limits to progress toward the hopes, dreams, and plans God has put on your heart. Ask yourself how you can devote yourself to "faithfulness goals" that are within your abilities. Ask how you can devote yourself further to your inner circles of friendship and perhaps a bit less to the periphery of your acquaintances. Consider how you could cut the clutter of your information inflow and focus on the sources of learning that matter most: the Bible, real-life friendships, prayer, high-quality books, and discerning the best way to spend your screen time.

I also encourage you to dream bigger, much bigger, than you could ever accomplish on your own as you consider the power of collaborating with other Christians around you and with the unlimited power of the Holy Spirit. Think, pray, and dream broadly, wildly, and beyond all you could ever ask or imagine, and then take faithful human-sized steps to find greater peace, joy, and effectiveness.

To him who is able to do immeasurably more than all we ask or imagine, according to his power that is at work within us, to him be glory in the church and in Christ Jesus throughout all generations, for ever and ever! Amen.

Ephesians 3:20–21

NOTES

Chapter 3: Humans Are unlike God

1. "Unanswered Prayers," track 7 on Garth Brooks, *No Fences*, Capitol Nashville, 1990.
2. I. A. Tjomsland, "Where Do We Go from Here?" in *Digest of Papers: The Gap between MSS Products and User Requirements, Fourth IEEE Symposium on Mass Storage Systems, April 15–17, 1980, Regency Hotel Denver* (New York: IEEE, 1980).

Chapter 4: The First Limit: Faithful Practices

1. Jaimie Duffek, "A Few Surprises in the Data behind Single-Sport and Multisport Athletes," *USA Today*, March 28, 2017, https://usatodayhss.com/2017/a-few-surprises-in-the-data -behind-single-sport-and-multisport-athletes.
2. Cal Newport, *Deep Work: Rules for Focused Success in a Distracted World* (New York: Grand Central, 2016), 136.

Chapter 5: The Second Limit: Circles of Friends

1. Robin Dunbar, "Coevolution of Neocortical Size, Group Size and Language in Humans," *Behavioral and Brain Sciences* 16, no. 4 (1993): 691, https://doi.org/10.1017/S0140525X00032325.
2. Robert E. Coleman, *The Master Plan of Evangelism* (Grand Rapids: Revell, 2010), 24–25.
3. Coleman, *The Master Plan of Evangelism*, 25.

Chapter 6: The Third Limit: Information

1. Mike Allen, "Sean Parker Unloads on Facebook: God Only Knows What It's Doing to Our Children's Brains," Axios, November 9, 2017, https://www.axios.com/sean-parker-unloads-on-facebook-2508036343.html.

2. Cal Newport, *Digital Minimalism: Choosing a Focused Life in a Noisy World* (New York: Penguin, 2019), 9.

3. "Netflix Commercial – SNL," Saturday Night Live, December 2, 2018, YouTube video, 2:25, https://www.youtube.com/watch?v=lqRQ5Y6OYi4.

4. Brandon Elrod, "Disciple-Making Task Force Report: Bible Engagement, Follow Up Key to Discipleship," North American Mission Board, June 21, 2018, https://www.namb.net/news/disciple-making-task-force-report-bible-engagement-follow-up-to-key-discussion/.

5. Wanda Thibodeaux, "Here's How Much Time People Actually Spend Reading Each Day," Inc., October 16, 2018, https://www.inc.com/wanda-thibodeaux/heres-how-much-time-people-actually-spend-reading-each-day.html.

6. H. Tankovska, "Daily Social Media Usage Worldwide 2012–2020," Statista, February 8, 2021, https://www.statista.com/statistics/433871/daily-social-media-usage-worldwide.

7. "How Many Chapters, Verses, and Words Are in the Bible?," Never Thirsty, accessed July 16, 2021, https://www.neverthirsty.org/bible-qa/qa-archives/question/how-many-chapters-verses-and-words-are-in-the-bible/.

8. Alison Dexter, "How Many Words Are in Harry Potter?," Word Counter, accessed July 16, 2021, https://wordcounter.io/blog/how-many-words-are-in-harry-potter/. "How Many Chapters, Verses, and Words Are in the Bible?," Never Thirsty, accessed July 16, 2021, https://www.neverthirsty.org/bible-qa/qa-archives/question/how-many-chapters-verses-and-words-are-in-the-bible/.

9. Akshay Jadhav and Prasad Kakade, "Display Market by Display

Type," Allied Market Research, September 2018, https://www
.alliedmarketresearch.com/display-market.

10. Jory MacKay, "Screen Time Stats 2019: Here's How Much You
Use Your Phone during the Workday," *RescueTime* (blog), March
21, 2019, https://blog.rescuetime.com/screen-time-stats-2018/.

Chapter 7: Limited but Not Alone: God's Presence

1. James D. Bratt, ed., *Abraham Kuyper: A Centennial Reader*
(Grand Rapids: Eerdmans, 1998), 488.

2. John Calvin, *Calvin: Institutes of the Christian Religion*, trans.
Ford Lewis Battles (Louisville, KY: Westminster John Knox
Press, 2001), 3.2.24 (1:570).

3. Calvin, 3.2.24 (1:570-571).

4. J. Todd Billings, *Union with Christ: Reframing Theology and
Ministry for the Church* (Grand Rapids: Baker Academic, 2011), 65.

5. Gordon Fee, *The First Epistle to the Corinthians* (Grand Rapids:
Eerdmans, 1987), 204.

Chapter 8: Limited but Not Alone: The Church

1. "Jimmy Wales," season 3, episode 72 of *The Colbert Report*,
Comedy Central, May 24, 2007, https://www.cc.com/video
/vylxk3/the-colbert-report-jimmy-wales.

2. Brandon Stosuy, "Sufjan Stevens on Art, the Internet, and, Yes,
the 50 States Project," Stereogum, December 1, 2009, https://
www.stereogum.com/103381/sufjan_stevens_on_art_internet
_and_yes_the_50_stat/news/.

3. "The Negotiation," season 3, episode 18 of *The Office*, first aired
2007, https://www.imdb.com/title/tt0983623/.

4. Wikipedia, s.v. "Wikipedia: Size of Wikipedia," last modified
July 13, 2021, https://en.wikipedia.org/wiki/Wikipedia:Size_of
_Wikipedia#Yearly_statistics.

5. Wikipedia, "Wikipedia Should Not Have Users," last modified
June 9, 2013, https://en.wikipedia.org/wiki
/Wikipedia:Wikipedia_should_not_have_users.